HOLY COMMUNION

A Service Book
for Use by the Minister

SUPPLEMENTAL WORSHIP RESOURCES 16

ABINGDON PRESS
Nashville
1987

HOLY COMMUNION: A Service Book for Use by the Minister

Copyright © 1987 by The United Methodist Publishing House

Library of Congress Cataloging-in-Publication Data

Hickman, Hoyt L. (Hoyt Leon), 1927-
Holy Communion.

(Supplemental worship resources; 16)
Bibliography: p.
1. Lord's Supper (Liturgy)—Texts. 2. United Methodist Church (U.S.)—Liturgy—Texts. 3. Methodist Church—Liturgy—Texts. I. Title. II. Series.
BX8338.H53 1987   264'.076036   86-28749

ISBN 0-687-17307-8

Excerpt from *Word and Table* copyright © 1976 by Abingdon. Used by permission.

The Sursum Corda, Sanctus, Benedictus, and the Lord's Prayer reprinted from *Prayers We Have in Common* copyright © 1970, 1971, and 1975 by International Consultation on English Texts. Used by permission.

The text of "Christ has died . . ." and the text of "Most loving God . . ." from the English translation of *The Roman Missal* © 1973, International Committee on English in the Liturgy, Inc. (ICEL); the English translation of the *Eucharistic Prayer of Hippolytus* © 1983, ICEL; excerpts from the English translation of *Eucharistic Prayer A* © 1986, ICEL. All rights reserved.

The prayer "Loving God . . ." also adapted in *The Service for the Lord's Day* (Supplemental Liturgical Resource 1). Copyright © 1984 The Westminster Press, Philadelphia, PA. Originally adapted with permission from a prayer in *An Australian Prayer Book* copyright © Anglican Church of Australia Trust Corporation.

Excerpts from *The Book of Services* copyright © 1985 by The United Methodist Publishing House. Used by permission.

Excerpts from *The Book of Worship for Church and Home* copyright © 1964, 1965 by Board of Publication of The United Methodist Church, Inc. Used by permission.

Excerpts reprinted from *The Handbook of the Christian Year*, copyright © 1986 by Abingdon Press. Used by permission.

Excerpts reprinted from *Ritual of The United Methodist Church* copyright © 1964 by Board of Publications of The Methodist Church, Incorporated. Used by permission.

Eucharistic Prayer 1 reprinted from *The Book of Alternative Services of the Anglican Church of Canada* copyright © 1985 by the General Synod of the Anglican Church of Canada. Used by permission.

Eucharistic Prayer VII reprinted from *A Sunday Liturgy for Optional Use in the United Church of Canada* © 1984 by The United Church of Canada. Used by permission.

The text of Service 23 and the post-communion prayer "Bountiful God, . . ." reprinted from *The Sacrament of the Lord's Supper: A New Text 1984* © 1984 and the prayer "Jesus Christ, the bread . . ." reprinted from *An Order of Worship* © 1968, both by Consultation on Church Union. Used by permission.

"The Eucharistic Liturgy of Lima" reprinted from *Baptism and Eucharist: Ecumenical Convergence in Celebration* copyright © The World Council of Churches. Jointly published by WCC Publications, Geneva, Switzerland, and Wm. B. Eerdmans Publishing Co. Used by permission of both the World Council of Churches and Wm. B. Eerdmans.

The Lord's Prayer from *The Discipline of The Evangelical United Brethren Church* copyright © 1959 by The Evangelical Press, Harrisburg, PA, and by The Otterbein Press, Dayton, OH.

Excerpt from the *Didache* reprinted from *Prayers of the Eucharist: Early and Reformed* © 1975 compilation, editorial matter and translation of original texts, R. C. D. Jasper and G. J. Cuming. Used by permission of Collins Publishers, London, and Oxford University Press, New York.

The text of "Through the broken bread . . ." reprinted by permission of United Church Press, from *The Hymnal of the United Church of Christ*. Copyright © 1974 United Church Press.

Scripture quotations on p. 59 are from the Revised Standard Version of the Bible, copyrighted 1946, 1952, © 1971, 1973 by the Division of Christian Education of the National Council of Churches of Christ in the U.S.A., and are used by permission.

MANUFACTURED BY THE PARTHENON PRESS AT
NASHVILLE, TENNESSEE, UNITED STATES OF AMERICA

CONTENTS

PREFACE

This collection of resources for Holy Communion is the sixteenth in the Supplemental Worship Resources (SWR) series developed and sponsored by the Section on Worship of the General Board of Discipleship of The United Methodist Church.

When The United Methodist Church was formed in 1968, *The Book of Discipline* provided (Par. 1388) that:

The hymnals of The United Methodist Church are the hymnals of The Evangelical United Brethren Church and *The Methodist Hymnal* [later retitled *The Book of Hymns*]; the Ritual of the Church is that contained in the *Book of Ritual* of The Evangelical United Brethren Church, 1959, and *The Book of Worship for Church and Home* of The Methodist Church.

It quickly became apparent, however, that there was a need for supplemental worship resources which, while not taking the place of these official resources, would provide alternatives that more fully reflect developments in the contemporary ecumenical church. The General Conferences of 1972 and 1976 authorized the General Board of Discipleship "to develop standards and resources for the conduct of public worship in the churches" (*The Book of Discipline* 1976, Par. 1316.2). The resulting series of Supplemental Worship Resources publications began with *The Sacrament of the Lord's Supper: An Alternate Text 1972* (SWR 1). During the next seven years seven other volumes were published, and in 1980 the service texts found in SWR 1 through 8 were revised and collected in the booklet *We Gather Together* (SWR 10), which was commended to local churches for trial use by the 1980 General Conference. *At the Lord's Table: A Communion Service Book for Use by the Minister* (SWR 9) was delayed in publication until 1981 and thus could incorporate the 1980 revisions of the Sacrament of the Lord's Supper as published in *We Gather Together*.

Further revisions were made in the services contained in *We Gather Together* as a result of trial use, and the revised services were submitted to the 1984 General Conference and officially adopted by it into the Ritual of The United Methodist Church. These official services were published in 1985 in *The Book of Services*.

There has proved to be a continuing need for SWR publications. SWR 11 through 13, published in 1981-83, supplement *The Book of Hymns*. SWR 14 and 15, published in 1984, contain occasional and seasonal services not found in *The Book of Services*.

Holy Communion (SWR 16) supplements *The Book of Services* in much the same way that *At the Lord's Table* (SWR 9) supplemented *We Gather Together* (SWR 10). The official Communion texts contained in *The Book of Services* were designed to be supplemented by other texts for alternative and seasonal use. The Great Thanksgiving, the words with breaking the bread and lifting the cup, the words with giving the bread and cup, the prayer after Communion, and the final blessing can appropriately be varied from one time and occasion to another. *Holy Communion* is designed to help the minister do this easily and effectively.

Like other publications in the SWR series, *Holy Communion* represents the work of many persons. The Section on Worship determined the specifications of the book and gave its approval and sponsorship to its publication. Hoyt L. Hickman of the Section on Worship staff was the editor of the manuscript and its writer, except where other authorship is indicated. From time to time during the writing he consulted with Don E. Saliers of Emory University, Laurence Hull Stookey of Wesley Theological Seminary, and James F. White of The University of Notre Dame. He also consulted with Thomas A. Langford III, Michael Williams, and Barbara Garcia of the staff of the General Board of Discipleship. The contributions of all these persons have been most helpful.

The members and staff of the Section on Worship, listed below, wish to thank the persons named above and the many others who have shared with us ideas regarding this book. Reactions and suggestions are welcomed by the Section on Worship, P.O. Box 840, Nashville, Tennessee 37202. We commend this book to the use of ministers and local churches in the hope that it will be useful in the worship of God and the proclamation of the gospel of Jesus Christ.

Stanley P. DePano, Chairperson,
Section on Worship
Bruce Blake
Nancy Brady
Carole Cotton-Winn
Gloster Current
D. S. Dharmapalan
Margarida Fortunato
Samuel Kaiser
Sue Kana-Mackey
Ruth Thomasson
Bishop Walter Underwood
Robert Bennett and Jerry W. Henry, representing the Fellowship of United Methodists in Worship, Music and Other Arts
Michael O'Donnell, representing the Order of Saint Luke
Ezra Earl Jones, General Secretary
Thomas A. Langford III, Assistant General Secretary
Hoyt L. Hickman, Director, Resource Development
Michael E. Williams, Staff

HOW TO USE THIS BOOK

This book is designed for the minister's use, not only in the study while planning services of Holy Communion, but also at the Lord's table while conducting services. It is designed to lie open on the Lord's table, with print large enough to be read by the minister while standing. Texts are included which are needed during the Service of the Table, or Holy Communion. It is assumed that the Service of the Word, centered in the pulpit, has already taken place.

The book is arranged so that page turns are minimized. The whole Service of the Table is usually printed on a two-page spread so that no page turn is needed. If the minister wishes to combine texts in ways other than that provided on the page spread, it is possible to turn after the Great Thanksgiving to page spread 58-59 and there have a wide choice of texts for later in the service. It is also possible to read the entire invitation-confession-pardon-peace-offering sequence on page spread 8-9.

It is important to examine the whole book carefully before using it in services. Since it is a supplement to *The Book of Services,* it is important to be familiar with that book as well. It will also be helpful to read *Companion to The Book of Services* (SWR 17), which is to be published soon by Abingdon and will contain an extensive commentary on these new official services.

If the congregation is using *The Book of Services,* the minister can easily use this book to provide more variety than can be found in *The Book of Services* itself. If the minister uses Service 1, the congregation can have the entire text in front of them in "A Service of Word and Table (Complete Text)" on page 19 ff. of *The Book of Services.* If the congregation uses "The Lord's Supper (Brief Text)" on pages 27 ff. of *The Book of Services* the minister can use Services 1 or 2, or any of the seasonal Services 4 through 13. Where there are four periods (. . . .) in the Great Thanksgiving, the people know that the minister may insert seasonal words. The minister can use Service 15 when the congregation uses "A Service of Christian Marriage" on pages 64 ff. of *The Book of Services* and Service 16 when the congregation uses "A Service of Death and Resurrection" on pages 75 ff. of *The Book of Services.*

Services 17 through 24 can be used if the people's responses and the cue lines are put in the worship bulletin. A model for this is found as "An Order of Holy Communion" on page 9 of this book and on pages 16 ff. of *The Book of Services.*

This format gives the congregation a fixed form of unison participation to which they can become accustomed, or which they can memorize, while providing the minister with flexibility. The congregation's responses are printed in **bold face type**. We encourage congregational singing of these responses, for they are more powerful sung than spoken. Musical settings of these responses are readily available and can easily be learned.

The minister is, of course, free not only to use any of the resources in this book or in *At the Lord's Table,* but to use or compose others as well. The minister will find helpful guidelines in "The Great Thanksgiving: Its Essential Elements" on page 9 of this book.

There is an added advantage to the flexibility provided by this book, in these days of theological and cultural diversity within the church. Many persons have raised questions regarding the theology implied by particular words and phrases. Often the persons most closely involved in the development of these services were agreed.

Nowhere was this more true than with the agonizing questions surrounding the use of masculine words in reference to God. The texts in *The Book of Services* as reproduced in this book represent the best resolution possible in our official Ritual at this time. Here the flexibility provided in this book is especially helpful. Services 17 through 23 provide a variety of language alternatives to the official Ritual, yet remain within the basic pattern. They also suggest ways in which the seasonal services can be altered, when a minister or congregation wishes.

The fact that this book deals with *words* used in Holy Communion should not obscure the fact that what is done in Holy Communion is primarily *action*. Great sensitivity to the importance of the nonverbal is called for in celebrating Holy Communion, and the reader's attention is called to the commentary on these actions to be found in *Companion to the Book of Services* (SWR 17). It is important that what is said and what is done in Holy Communion be carefully thought through so that they will be in harmony with one another.

There are four basic actions in Holy Communion: (1) taking the bread and cup, (2) giving thanks over the bread and cup, (3) breaking the bread, and (4) giving the bread and cup. Of these, all but the second are nonverbal, though they may be accompanied with appropriate words. Since the first and third of these actions are very brief and preliminary to the second and fourth, we might see these steps as two: (1) taking the bread and cup and giving thanks over them, and (2) breaking the bread and giving the bread and cup to one another. The Great Thanksgiving (giving thanks over the bread and cup) is the prayer that accompanies taking the bread and cup; no other form of words is necessary. A variety of words appropriate for use with breaking the bread and giving the bread and cup are provided, as are a variety of prayers after Communion and final blessings (benedictions).

The minister's actions at the Lord's table will be more expressive and have greater sign value to the congregation if the minister stands behind the Lord's table, facing the Lord's people. Standing is the biblical and traditional posture for a prayer of praise and thanksgiving. Taking the bread and cup, breaking the bread, and giving the bread and cup are all more eloquent actions when done standing and facing the family of God.

What is done in Holy Communion is an enactment of the gospel itself, and it summarizes in the most powerful way all that we believe and all that we teach.

THE CALENDAR OF THE CHRISTIAN YEAR

ADVENT SEASON
   First Sunday of Advent
      to Fourth Sunday of Advent (4)*

CHRISTMAS SEASON
   Christmas Eve/Day (5)
   First Sunday after Christmas (5)
   New Year's Eve/Day (6, 5)
   Second Sunday after Christmas** (5)
   Epiphany (6)

SEASON AFTER EPIPHANY
   First Sunday after Epiphany
      (Baptism of the Lord) (6)
   Second Sunday after Epiphany to
      Eighth Sunday after Epiphany**
      (1,2,6)
   Last Sunday after Epiphany
      (Transfiguration Sunday) (1,2,6)

LENTEN SEASON
   Ash Wednesday (7)
   First Sunday of Lent
      to Fifth Sunday of Lent (7,8)
   Holy Week
      Passion/Palm Sunday (8)
      Monday in Holy Week (8)
      Tuesday in Holy Week (8)
      Wednesday in Holy Week (8)
      Holy Thursday (9)

Good Friday
Holy Saturday

EASTER SEASON
   Easter Vigil (10)
   Easter (10)
   Second Sunday of Easter
      to Sixth Sunday of Easter (10)
   Ascension
      (Sixth Thursday of Easter) (10)
   Seventh Sunday of Easter (10)
   Pentecost (11)

SEASON AFTER PENTECOST
(UNITED METHODIST KINGDOMTIDE)
   Trinity Sunday
      (First Sunday after Pentecost) (1)
   Second Sunday after Pentecost
      to 27th Sunday after Pentecost**
      (1,12)
   Christ the King
      (Last Sunday after Pentecost) (12)
   All Saints (November 1 or
      First Sunday in November) (13)
   Thanksgiving Day (14)

* Numbers in parentheses refer to services in this book particularly appropriate to the day. Services 1-3 and 17-24 are appropriate for use throughout the year.
**The number of Sundays occurring after Christmas, Epiphany, and Pentecost varies from year to year.

A BASIC PATTERN OF WORSHIP

The Entrance
The people come together in the Lord's name. There may be greetings, music and song, prayer and praise.

Proclamation and Response
The Scriptures are opened to the people through the reading of lessons, preaching, witnessing, music, or other arts and media. Interspersed may be psalms, anthems, and hymns.

Responses to God's Word include acts of commitment and faith with offerings of concerns, prayers, gifts, and service for the world and for one another.

Thanksgiving and Communion
In services with Communion, the actions of Jesus in the Upper Room are reenacted:
    taking the bread and cup,
    giving thanks over the bread and cup,
    breaking the bread, and
    giving the bread and cup.
In services without Communion, thanks are given for God's mighty acts in Jesus Christ.

Sending Forth
The people are sent into ministry with the Lord's blessing.

AN OUTLINE OF WORSHIP WITH HOLY COMMUNION

Gathering
Greeting
Hymn of Praise
Prayer of the Day,
    Confession and Pardon,
    and/or Litany
[Act of Praise]
[Praise for Illumination]
Scripture Lesson
[Psalm]
[Scripture Lesson]
Hymn or Song
Gospel Lesson
Sermon
Response to the Word
Concerns and Prayers
[Confession and Pardon]
The Peace
Offering
Taking the Bread and Cup
The Great Thanksgiving
Breaking the Bread
Giving the Bread and Cup
Hymn or Song
Dismissal with Blessing
Going Forth

PREPARATORY TO HOLY COMMUNION

Christ our Lord invites to his table
all who love him,
who earnestly repent of their sin
and seek to live in peace with one another.
Therefore, let us confess our sin
before God and one another.

**Merciful God,
we confess that often we have failed
to be an obedient Church.
We have not done your will,
we have broken your law,
we have rebelled against your love,
we have not loved our neighbors, and
we have not heard the cry of the needy.
Forgive us, we pray.
Free us for joyful obedience,
through Jesus Christ our Lord. Amen.**

All pray in silence.

Minister to people:
Hear the good news:
"Christ died for us
while we were yet sinners;
that proves God's love toward us."
In the name of Jesus Christ,
you are forgiven.

People to minister:
**In the name of Jesus Christ,
you are forgiven.**

Minister and people:
Glory to God. Amen.

Let us offer one another
signs of reconciliation and love.

*All exchange signs and words
of God's peace.*

As forgiven and reconciled people,
let us offer ourselves and our gifts to God.

*The offering is received
and brought to the Lord's table.*

Let us confess our sins
against God and our neighbor.

Silence may be kept.

**Most merciful God,
we confess that we have sinned against you
in thought, word, and deed,
by what we have done,
and by what we have left undone.
We have not loved you
with our whole heart;
we have not loved our neighbors
as ourselves.
We are truly sorry and we humbly repent.
For the sake of your Son Jesus Christ,
have mercy on us and forgive us;
that we may delight in your will,
and walk in your ways,
to the glory of your Name. Amen.**

Almighty God have mercy on you,
forgive you all your sins
through our Lord Jesus Christ,
strengthen you in all goodness,
and by the power of the Holy Spirit
keep you in eternal life.

Amen.

The peace of the Lord be always with you.

And also with you.

*Then the minister(s) and people
may greet one another
in the name of the Lord.*

*The minister may begin the offering
with a sentence of Scripture.*

*The offering is received
and brought to the Lord's table.*

AN ORDER OF HOLY COMMUNION

The bread and wine are brought
by representatives of the people
to the Lord's table,
or are uncovered if already in place.
The minister takes the bread and cup,
and the bread and wine are prepared
for the meal.

The Great Thanksgiving is then prayed
according to the following pattern:

The Lord be with you.
And also with you.
Lift up your hearts.
We lift them to the Lord.
Let us give thanks to the Lord our God.
It is right to give our thanks and praise.

The minister gives thanks
appropriate to the occasion,
remembering God's acts of salvation,
and concludes:
And so, with your people on earth
and all the company of heaven
we praise your name
and join their unending hymn:

Holy, holy, holy Lord,
God of power and might,
heaven and earth are full of your glory.
Hosanna in the highest.
Blessed is he
who comes in the name of the Lord.
Hosanna in the highest.

The minister continues the thanksgiving.
The institution of the Lord's Supper is recalled.
The minister concludes:

And so, in remembrance
of these your mighty acts in Jesus Christ,
we offer ourselves

in praise and thanksgiving
as a holy and living sacrifice,
in union with Christ's offering for us,
as we proclaim the mystery of faith.

Christ has died,
Christ is risen,
Christ will come again.

The minister then invokes
the present work of the Holy Spirit
and then praises the Trinity, concluding:
All honor and glory is yours,
Almighty Father *(God)*, now and for ever.

Amen.

And now,
with the confidence of children of God,
let us pray:

All pray the Lord's Prayer.

The minister breaks the bread in silence,
or with appropriate words.
The minister then lifts the cup in silence,
or with appropriate words.
The bread and wine are given to the people,
with these or other words being exchanged:
The body of Christ, given for you. **Amen.**
The blood of Christ, given for you. **Amen.**

The congregation sings hymns
while the bread and cup are given.

When all have received,
the Lord's table is put in order.

The minister or congregation
may give thanks after Communion.

A hymn or song may be sung.

The people are dismissed with the blessing.

THE GREAT THANKSGIVING: ITS ESSENTIAL ELEMENTS

There is a definite structure to the way Christians give thanks in the Lord's Supper. This structure is apparent in Great Thanksgivings from the early third century to the present day. It appears in documents written before the canon of New Testament scriptures was finally determined and is at least as old as any creed. This very universality of the way Christians give thanks is a mirror of the church's perception of its relationship to God.

The Great Thanksgiving is a hymn of praise and a creed as much as it is a prayer. It is trinitarian, though it is addressed throughout to the first Person of the Trinity. It begins in thanksgiving to God the Father, narrates the work of God the Christ, and invokes the Father to send God the Holy Spirit for our benefit. The concluding doxology, though addressed to God the Father, ties together the trinitarian nature of the whole prayer.

The Great Thanksgiving opens with (1) a *dialogue* of greeting between the presiding minister and people and invites them to join in the giving of thanks, just as we might introduce grace before an ordinary meal.

Then comes (2) a joyful thanksgiving called the *preface*, which usually recites either a specific work of Christ (varying according to season or occasion) or a general narration of salvation history.

This thankful recalling of God's mighty acts is punctuated by (3) a *congregational acclamation* of praise: "Holy, holy, holy" (*Sanctus*) from Isaiah 6:3 and Revelation 4:8 and "Blessed is he who comes in the name of the Lord" (*Benedictus qui venit*) from Psalm 118:26 and Matthew 21:9. In some Christian traditions, God's mighty acts under the old covenant are recited before this acclamation, and the new covenant follows. In other traditions, this acclamation comes either at the beginning or at the end of the whole recitation.

This is followed and culminated by (4) the *words of institution*—the commemoration of the events in which Jesus instituted the Lord's Supper. Some traditions locate the words of institution at their chronological place in the recitation of salvation history, but in any event these words are not neglected.

Then occurs (5) the remembering *(anamnesis)* before God of what Jesus Christ has done as we offer this memorial of his sacrifice *(oblation)*. Usually this segment of the prayer refers concisely to Christ's death, resurrection, and ascension, offering these before God for our benefit.

Many recent liturgies employ a *memorial acclamation,* such as "Christ has died, Christ is risen, Christ will come again," after the words of institution or after the *anamnesis* and *oblation.*

Next comes (6) an invocation *(epiclesis)* in which God is asked to send the Holy Spirit upon the gifts and on the assembled congregation. Benefits desired from communion are prayed for. Intercessions for the living and dead have sometimes occurred at this point.

Triumphantly and joyfully all concludes with (7) a trinitarian *doxology* and *amen.* The doxology sums up in praise the trinitarian theme of the whole prayer.

Frequently (8) *The Lord's Prayer* follows as a congregational act in which we address with familiar confidence the God who has done all these wonderful things simply as "Our Father."

The way Christians give thanks reflects the very nature of Christianity in two ways. First, the Great Thanksgiving is basically a creedal act combining doxology and theology in a joyful statement of belief. Indeed for most of its history much of Western Christianity found any other creedal statement redundant at the Lord's Supper. Second, the Great Thanksgiving represents the whole biblical mentality of giving thanks by recital of what God has done. Every time we "do this" we thankfully show forth what God has done in Christ and testify to God's accessibility through recital of what God has done for us. It is a practice older than the written gospels and epistles and directly in line with Christ's use of the Passover occasion to combine reenactment and presence in a new covenant.

HIPPOLYTUS: *THE APOSTOLIC TRADITION*

The Lord be with you.
And also with you.
Lift up your hearts.
We lift them to the Lord.
Let us give thanks to the Lord [our God].
**It is right
to give [our] thanks and praise.**

We give you thanks, O God,
through your beloved Servant, Jesus Christ.
It is he whom you have sent
in these last times
to save us and redeem us,
and be the messenger of your will.
He is your Word,
inseparable from you,
through whom you made all things
and in whom you take delight.

You sent him from heaven
into the Virgin's womb,
where he was conceived, and took flesh.
Born of the Holy Spirit and the Virgin,
he was revealed as your Son.

In fulfillment of your will
he stretched out his hands in suffering
to release from suffering
those who place their hope in you,
and so he won for you a holy people.

Of his own free choice
he was handed over to his passion
in order to make an end of death
and to shatter the chains of the evil one;
to trample underfoot the powers of hell
and to lead the righteous into light;
to establish the boundaries of death
and to manifest the resurrection.

And so he took bread
and gave you thanks, saying:

Take, and eat:
this is my body
which will be broken for you.
In the same way he took the cup, saying:
This is my blood
which will be shed for you.
When you do this, you do it in memory of me.

Remembering therefore
his death and resurrection,
we offer you this bread and cup,
thankful that you have counted us worthy
to stand in your presence
and show you priestly service.

We entreat you to send your Holy Spirit
upon the offering of the holy Church.
Gather into one
all who share in these sacred mysteries,
filling them with the Holy Spirit
and confirming their faith in the truth,
that together we may praise you
and give you glory
through your Servant, Jesus Christ.

All glory and honor is yours,
Father and Son,
with the Holy Spirit
in the holy Church,
now and for ever.

Amen.

This is the Great Thanksgiving from *The Apostolic Tradition* of Hippolytus, which dates from about A.D. 215 and is the oldest text in existence that is undoubtedly a liturgy of Holy Communion. Since Hippolytus of Rome was very conservative in resisting innovations and was setting down in *The Apostolic Tradition* "the tradition which has remained until now," we may take it as a witness to the practice in Rome some fifty years earlier. It agrees quite closely with the account of the order of worship (without text) given by Justin Martyr in Rome about A.D. 155.

The Lord be with you.
And also with you.
Lift up your hearts.
We lift them to the Lord.
Let us give thanks to the Lord our God.
It is right to give our thanks and praise.

It is right, and a good and joyful thing,
always and everywhere
to give thanks to you, Father Almighty,
Creator of heaven and earth.

You formed us in your image
and breathed into us the breath of life.
When we turned away, and our love failed,
your love remained steadfast.
You delivered us from captivity,
made covenant to be our sovereign God,
and spoke to us through your prophets.

And so, with your people on earth
and all the company of heaven,
we praise your name
and join their unending hymn:

Holy, holy, holy Lord,
God of power and might,
heaven and earth are full of your glory.
Hosanna in the highest.
Blessed is he
who comes in the name of the Lord.
Hosanna in the highest.

Holy are you,
and blessed is your Son Jesus Christ.
Your Spirit anointed him
to preach good news to the poor,
to proclaim release to the captives
and recovering of sight to the blind,
to set at liberty those who are oppressed,
and to announce that the time had come
when you would save your people.
He healed the sick, fed the hungry,
and ate with sinners.

By the baptism
of his suffering, death, and resurrection
you gave birth to your Church,

delivered us from slavery to sin and death,
and made with us a new covenant
by water and the Spirit.
When the Lord Jesus ascended,
he promised to be with us always,
in the power of your Word and Holy Spirit.

On the night
in which he gave himself up for us
he took bread,
gave thanks to you,
broke the bread,
gave it to his disciples, and said:
"Take, eat;
this is my body which is given for you.
Do this in remembrance of me."

When the supper was over
he took the cup,
gave thanks to you,
gave it to his disciples, and said:
"Drink from this, all of you;
this is my blood of the new covenant,
poured out for you and for many
for the forgiveness of sins.
Do this, as often as you drink it,
in remembrance of me."

And so, in remembrance
of these your mighty acts in Jesus Christ,
we offer ourselves
in praise and thanksgiving
as a holy and living sacrifice,
in union with Christ's offering for us,
as we proclaim the mystery of faith.

Christ has died,
Christ is risen,
Christ will come again.

Pour out your Holy Spirit on us,
gathered here,
and on these gifts of bread and wine.
Make them be for us
the body and blood of Christ,
that we may be for the world
the body of Christ, redeemed by his blood.

By your Spirit make us one with Christ,
one with each other,
and one in ministry to all the world,
until Christ comes in final victory
and we feast at his heavenly banquet.

Through your Son Jesus Christ,
with the Holy Spirit in your holy Church,
all honor and glory is yours,
Almighty Father, now and for ever.

Amen.

And now,
with the confidence of children of God,
let us pray:

**Our Father in heaven,
hallowed be your Name,
your kingdom come,
your will be done,
on earth as in heaven.
Give us today our daily bread.
Forgive us our sins
as we forgive those who sin against us.
Save us from the time of trial,
and deliver us from evil.
For the kingdom, the power, and the glory
are yours now and for ever. Amen.**

*The minister breaks the bread in silence,
or while saying:*
Because there is one loaf,
we, who are many, are one body,
for we all partake of the one loaf.
The bread which we break
is a sharing in the body of Christ.

*The minister lifts the cup in silence,
or while saying:*
The cup over which we give thanks
is a sharing in the blood of Christ.

*The bread and wine are given to the people,
with these or other words being exchanged:*

The body of Christ, given for you. **Amen.**
The blood of Christ, given for you. **Amen.**

*The congregation sings hymns
while the bread and cup are given.*

*When all have received,
the Lord's table is put in order.*

*One of the following prayers
is then offered by the minister or by all:*
**Eternal God,
we give you thanks for this holy mystery
in which you have given yourself to us.
Grant that we may go into the world
in the strength of your Spirit,
to give ourselves for others,
in the name of Jesus Christ our Lord.
Amen.**

**Loving God, we thank you
that you have fed us in this Sacrament,
united us with Christ,
and given us a foretaste
of the heavenly banquet
in your eternal kingdom.
Send us out in the power of your Spirit
to live and work to your praise and glory,
in Jesus' name. Amen.**

A hymn or song may be sung.

The people are dismissed with the blessing:
Go forth in peace.
The grace of the Lord Jesus Christ,
and the love of God,
and the communion of the Holy Spirit
be with you all.
Amen.

Service 1 is intended for use throughout the year,
especially during the Season after Epiphany and the
Season after Pentecost.

For alternative texts following this Great Thanksgiving, turn to page 58.

The Lord be with you.
And also with you.
Lift up your hearts.
We lift them to the Lord.
Let us give thanks to the Lord our God.
It is right to give our thanks and praise.

It is right, and a good and joyful thing,
always and everywhere
to give thanks to you, Father Almighty,
Creator of heaven and earth.

And so, with your people on earth
and all the company of heaven
we praise your name
and join their unending hymn:

Holy, holy, holy Lord,
God of power and might,
heaven and earth are full of your glory.
Hosanna in the highest.
Blessed is he
who comes in the name of the Lord.
Hosanna in the highest.

Holy are you,
and blessed is your Son Jesus Christ.
By the baptism
of his suffering, death, and resurrection
you gave birth to your Church,
delivered us from slavery to sin and death,
and made with us a new covenant
by water and the Spirit.

On the night
in which he gave himself up for us
he took bread,
gave thanks to you,
broke the bread,
gave it to his disciples, and said:
"Take, eat;
this is my body which is given for you.
Do this in remembrance of me."

When the supper was over
he took the cup,
gave thanks to you,
gave it to his disciples, and said:

"Drink from this, all of you;
this is my blood of the new covenant,
poured out for you and for many
for the forgiveness of sins.
Do this, as often as you drink it,
in remembrance of me."

And so, in remembrance
of these your mighty acts in Jesus Christ,
we offer ourselves
in praise and thanksgiving
as a holy and living sacrifice,
in union with Christ's offering for us,
as we proclaim the mystery of faith.

Christ has died,
Christ is risen,
Christ will come again.

Pour out your Holy Spirit on us,
gathered here,
and on these gifts of bread and wine.
Make them be for us
the body and blood of Christ,
that we may be for the world
the body of Christ, redeemed by his blood.

By your Spirit make us one with Christ,
one with each other,
and one in ministry to all the world,
until Christ comes in final victory,
and we feast at his heavenly banquet.

Through your Son Jesus Christ,
with the Holy Spirit in your holy Church,
all honor and glory is yours,
Almighty Father, now and for ever.

Amen.

And now,
with the confidence of children of God,
let us pray:

Our Father . . .

Continue on page 13, 15, or 58.

Services 2 and 3 are intended for use in home or
hospital settings or in other situations where brevity
is essential.

Lift up your heart(s)
and give thanks to the Lord our God.

Father Almighty,
Creator of heaven and earth,
you made us in your image,
to love and to be loved.
When we turned away, and our love failed,
your love remained steadfast.
By the suffering, death, and resurrection
of your only Son Jesus Christ
you delivered us
from slavery to sin and death
and made with us a new covenant
by water and the Spirit.

On the night
in which he gave himself up for us
he took bread,
gave thanks to you,
broke the bread,
gave it to his disciples, and said:
"Take, eat;
this is my body which is given for you.
Do this in remembrance of me."

When the supper was over
he took the cup,
gave thanks to you,
gave it to his disciples, and said:
"Drink from this, all of you;
for this is my blood of the new covenant,
poured out for you and for many
for the forgiveness of sins.
Do this, as often as you drink it,
in remembrance of me."

And so, in remembrance
of these your mighty acts in Jesus Christ,
we offer ourselves
in praise and thanksgiving
as a holy and living sacrifice,
in union with Christ's offering for us.

Pour out your Holy Spirit on us
and on these gifts of bread and wine.
Make them be for us
the body and blood of Christ,
that we may be for the world
the body of Christ, redeemed by his blood.

By your Spirit make us one with Christ,
one with each other,
and one in ministry to all the world,
until Christ comes in final victory,
and we feast at his heavenly banquet.

Through your Son Jesus Christ,
with the Holy Spirit in your holy Church,
all honor and glory is yours,
Almighty Father, now and for ever.

Amen.

And now,
with the confidence of children of God,
let us pray:

**Our Father in heaven,
hallowed be your Name,
your kingdom come,
your will be done,
on earth as in heaven.
Give us today our daily bread.
Forgive us our sins
as we forgive those who sin against us.
Save us from the time of trial,
and deliver us from evil.
For the kingdom, the power, and the glory
are yours, now and for ever. Amen.**

The minister breaks the bread.

*The bread and wine are given to the people,
with these or other words being exchanged:*
The body of Christ, given for you. **Amen.**
The blood of Christ, given for you. **Amen.**

*When all have received,
the Lord's table is put in order.*

Thanks may be given after Communion.

A hymn or song may be sung.

The minister gives the blessing:
The grace of the Lord Jesus Christ,
and the love of God,
and the communion of the Holy Spirit
be with you all. **Amen.**

The Lord be with you.
And also with you.
Lift up your hearts.
We lift them to the Lord.
Let us give thanks to the Lord our God.
It is right to give our thanks and praise.

It is right, and a good and joyful thing,
always and everywhere
to give thanks to you, Father Almighty,
Creator of heaven and earth.

You formed us in your image
and breathed into us the breath of life.
When we turned away, and our love failed,
your love remained steadfast.
You delivered us from captivity,
made covenant to be our sovereign God,
and spoke to us through your prophets,
who looked for that day
when justice shall roll down like waters
and righteousness
like an ever-flowing stream,
when nation shall not lift up sword
against nation,
neither shall they learn war any more.

And so, with your people on earth
and all the company of heaven,
we praise your name
and join their unending hymn:

Holy, holy, holy Lord,
God of power and might,
heaven and earth are full of your glory.
Hosanna in the highest.
Blessed is he
who comes in the name of the Lord.
Hosanna in the highest.

Holy are you,
and blessed is your Son Jesus Christ,
whom you sent in the fullness of time
to be a light to the nations.
You scatter the proud
in the imagination of their hearts
and have mercy on those who fear you
from generation to generation.

You put down the mighty
from their thrones
and exalt those of low degree.
You fill the hungry with good things,
and the rich you send empty away.
Your own Son came among us as a servant,
to be Emmanuel, your presence with us.
He humbled himself
in obedience to your will
and freely accepted death on a cross.
By the baptism
of his suffering, death, and resurrection
you gave birth to your Church,
delivered us from slavery to sin and death,
and made with us a new covenant
by water and the Spirit.

On the night
in which he gave himself up for us
he took bread,
gave thanks to you,
broke the bread,
gave it to his disciples, and said:
"Take, eat;
this is my body which is given for you.
Do this in remembrance of me."

When the supper was over
he took the cup,
gave thanks to you,
gave it to his disciples, and said:
"Drink from this, all of you;
this is my blood of the new covenant,
poured out for you and for many
for the forgiveness of sins.
Do this, as often as you drink it,
in remembrance of me."

And so, in remembrance
of these your mighty acts in Jesus Christ,
we offer ourselves
in praise and thanksgiving
as a holy and living sacrifice,
in union with Christ's offering for us,
as we proclaim the mystery of faith.

Christ has died,
Christ is risen,
Christ will come again.

Pour out your Holy Spirit on us,
gathered here,
and on these gifts of bread and wine.
Make them be for us
the body and blood of Christ,
that we may be for the world
the body of Christ, redeemed by his blood.

By your Spirit make us one with Christ,
one with each other,
and one in ministry to all the world,
until Christ comes in final victory
and we feast at his heavenly banquet.

Through your Son Jesus Christ,
with the Holy Spirit in your holy Church,
all honor and glory is yours,
Almighty Father, now and for ever.

Amen.

And now,
with the confidence of children of God,
let us pray:

**Our Father in heaven,
hallowed be your Name,
your kingdom come,
your will be done
on earth as in heaven.
Give us today our daily bread.
Forgive us our sins
as we forgive those who sin against us.
Save us from the time of trial,
and deliver us from evil.
For the kingdom, the power, and the glory
are yours now and for ever.
Amen.**

*The minister breaks the bread in silence,
or while saying:*
Because there is one loaf,
we, who are many, are one body,
for we all partake of the one loaf.
The bread which we break
is a sharing in the body of Christ.

*The minister lifts the cup in silence,
or while saying:*
The cup over which we give thanks
is a sharing in the blood of Christ.

*The bread and wine are given to the people,
with these or other words being exchanged:*
The body of Christ, given for you. **Amen.**
The blood of Christ, given for you. **Amen.**

*The congregation sings hymns
while the bread and cup are given.*

*When all have received,
the Lord's table is put in order.*

*One of the following prayers
is then offered by the minister or by all:*
**Eternal God,
we give you thanks for this holy mystery
in which you have given yourself to us.
Grant that we may go into the world
in the strength of your Spirit,
to give ourselves to others,
in the name of Jesus Christ our Lord.
Amen.**

**Loving God, we thank you
that you have fed us in this Sacrament,
united us with Christ,
and given us a foretaste
of the heavenly banquet
in your eternal kingdom.
Send us out in the power of your Spirit
to live and work to your praise and glory,
in Jesus' name. Amen.**

A hymn or song may be sung.

The people are dismissed with the blessing:
Go forth in peace.
The grace of the Lord Jesus Christ,
and the love of God,
and the communion of the Holy Spirit
be with you all. **Amen.**

For alternative texts following this Great Thanksgiving, turn to page 58.

The Lord be with you.
And also with you.
Lift up your hearts.
We lift them to the Lord.
Let us give thanks to the Lord our God.
It is right to give our thanks and praise.

It is right, and a good and joyful thing
always and everywhere
to give thanks to you, Father Almighty,
Creator of heaven and earth.

You created light out of darkness
and brought forth life on the earth.
You formed us in your image
and breathed into us the breath of life.
When we turned away, and our love failed,
your love remained steadfast.
You delivered us from captivity,
made covenant to be our sovereign God,
and spoke to us through your prophets.
In the fullness of time
you gave your only Son Jesus Christ
to be our Savior,
and at his birth the angels sang
glory to you in the highest
and peace to your people on earth.

And so, with your people on earth
and all the company of heaven,
we praise your name
and join their unending hymn:

Holy, holy, holy Lord,
God of power and might,
heaven and earth are full of your glory.
Hosanna in the highest.
Blessed is he
who comes in the name of the Lord.
Hosanna in the highest.

Holy are you,
and blessed is your Son Jesus Christ.
As Mary and Joseph went
from Galilee to Bethlehem
and there found no room,
so Jesus went
from Galilee to Jerusalem
and was despised and rejected.

As in the poverty of a stable
Jesus was born,
so, by the baptism
of his suffering, death, and resurrection
you gave birth to your Church,
delivered us from slavery to sin and death,
and made with us a new covenant
by water and the Spirit.

As your Word became flesh,
born of woman,
on that night long ago,
so, on the night
in which he gave himself up for us
he took bread,
gave thanks to you,
broke the bread,
gave it to his disciples, and said:
"Take, eat;
this is my body which is given for you.
Do this in remembrance of me."

When the supper was over
he took the cup,
gave thanks to you,
gave it to his disciples, and said:
"Drink from this, all of you;
this is my blood of the new covenant,
poured out for you and for many
for the forgiveness of sins.
Do this, as often as you drink it,
in remembrance of me."

And so, in remembrance
of these your mighty acts in Jesus Christ,
we offer ourselves
in praise and thanksgiving
as a holy and living sacrifice,
in union with Christ's offering for us,
as we proclaim the mystery of faith.

Christ has died,
Christ is risen,
Christ will come again.

Pour out your Holy Spirit on us,
gathered here,
and on these gifts of bread and wine.

Make them be for us
the body and blood of Christ,
that we may be for the world
the body of Christ, redeemed by his blood.

By your Spirit make us one with Christ,
one with each other,
and one in ministry to all the world,
until Christ comes in final victory
and we feast at his heavenly banquet.

Through your Son Jesus Christ,
with the Holy Spirit in your holy Church,
all honor and glory is yours,
Almighty Father, now and for ever.

Amen.

And now,
with the confidence of children of God,
let us pray:

**Our Father in heaven,
hallowed be your Name,
your kingdom come,
your will be done
on earth as in heaven.
Give us today our daily bread.
Forgive us our sins
as we forgive those who sin against us.
Save us from the time of trial
and deliver us from evil.
For the kingdom, the power, and the glory
are yours now and for ever. Amen.**

*The minister breaks the bread in silence,
or while saying:*
Because there is one loaf,
we, who are many, are one body,
for we all partake of the one loaf.
The bread which we break
is a sharing in the body of Christ.

*The minister lifts the cup in silence,
or while saying:*
The cup over which we give thanks
is a sharing in the blood of Christ.

*The bread and wine are given to the people,
with these or other words being exchanged:*
The body of Christ, given for you. **Amen.**
The blood of Christ, given for you. **Amen.**

*The congregation sings hymns
while the bread and cup are given.*

*When all have received,
The Lord's table is put in order.*

*One of the following prayers
is then offered by the minister or by all:*
**Eternal God,
we give you thanks for this holy mystery
in which you have given yourself to us.
Grant that we may go into the world
in the strength of your Spirit,
to give ourselves to others,
in the name of Jesus Christ our Lord.
Amen.**

**Loving God, we thank you
that you have fed us in this Sacrament,
united us with Christ,
and given us a foretaste
of the heavenly banquet
in your eternal kingdom.
Send us out in the power of your Spirit
to live and work to your praise and glory,
in Jesus' name. Amen.**

A hymn or song may be sung.

The people are dismissed with the blessing:
Go forth in peace.
The grace of the Lord Jesus Christ,
and the love of God,
and the communion of the Holy Spirit
be with you all.

Amen.

For alternative texts following this Great Thanksgiving, turn to page 58.

The Lord be with you.
And also with you.
Lift up your hearts.
We lift them to the Lord.
Let us give thanks to the Lord our God.
It is right to give our thanks and praise.

It is right, and a good and joyful thing,
always and everywhere
to give thanks to you, Father Almighty,
Creator of heaven and earth.

Before the mountains were brought forth
or you had formed the earth,
from everlasting to everlasting
you alone are God.
You created light out of darkness
and brought forth life on the earth.
You formed us in your image
and breathed into us the breath of life.
When we turned away, and our love failed,
your love remained steadfast.
You delivered us from captivity,
made covenant to be our sovereign God,
and spoke to us through your prophets.

And so, with your people on earth
and all the company of heaven,
we praise your name
and join their unending hymn:

Holy, holy, holy Lord,
God of power and might,
heaven and earth are full of your glory.
Hosanna in the highest.
Blessed is he
who comes in the name of the Lord.
Hosanna in the highest.

Holy are you,
and blessed is your Son Jesus Christ,
in whom you have revealed yourself,
our light and our salvation.

[You sent a star to guide wise men
to where the Christ was born;
and your signs and witnesses
in every age and through all the world

have led your people from far places
to his light.]

[In his baptism and in table fellowship
he took his place with sinners.
Your Spirit anointed him
to preach good news to the poor,
to proclaim release to the captives
and recovering of sight to the blind,
to set at liberty those who are oppressed,
and to announce that the time had come
when you would save your people.]

By the baptism
of his suffering, death, and resurrection
you gave birth to your Church,
delivered us from slavery to sin and death,
and made with us a new covenant
by water and the Spirit.

On the night
in which he gave himself up for us
he took bread,
gave thanks to you,
broke the bread,
gave it to his disciples, and said:
"Take, eat;
this is my body which is given for you.
Do this in remembrance of me."

When the supper was over
he took the cup,
gave thanks to you,
gave it to his disciples, and said:
"Drink from this, all of you;
this is my blood of the new covenant,
poured out for you and for many
for the forgiveness of sins.
Do this, as often as you drink it,
in remembrance of me."

And so, in remembrance
of these your mighty acts in Jesus Christ,
we offer ourselves
in praise and thanksgiving
as a holy and living sacrifice,
in union with Christ's offering for us,
as we proclaim the mystery of faith.

**Christ has died,
Christ is risen,
Christ will come again.**

Pour out your Holy Spirit on us,
gathered here,
and on these gifts of bread and wine.
Make them be for us
the body and blood of Christ,
that we may be for the world
the body of Christ, redeemed by his blood.

By your Spirit make us one with Christ,
one with each other,
and one in ministry to all the world,
until Christ comes in final victory
and we feast at his heavenly banquet.

Through your Son Jesus Christ,
with the Holy Spirit in your holy Church,
all honor and glory is yours,
Almighty Father, now and for ever.

Amen.

And now,
with the confidence of children of God,
let us pray:

**Our Father in heaven,
hallowed be your Name,
your kingdom come,
your will be done
on earth as in heaven.
Give us today our daily bread.
Forgive us our sins
as we forgive those who sin against us.
Save us from the time of trial,
and deliver us from evil.
For the kingdom, the power, and the glory
are yours now and for ever. Amen.**

*The minister breaks the bread in silence,
or while saying:*
Because there is one loaf,
we, who are many, are one body,
for we all partake of the one loaf.
The bread which we break
is a sharing in the body of Christ.

*The minister lifts the cup in silence,
or while saying:*
The cup over which we give thanks
is a sharing in the blood of Christ.

*The bread and wine are given to the people,
with these or other words being exchanged:*
The body of Christ, given for you. **Amen.**
The blood of Christ, given for you. **Amen.**

*The congregation sings hymns
while the bread and cup are given.*

*When all have received,
the Lord's table is put in order.*

*One of the following prayers is then offered
by the minister or by all:*
**Eternal God,
we give you thanks for this holy mystery
in which you have given yourself to us.
Grant that we may go into the world
in the strength of your Spirit,
to give ourselves to others,
in the name of Jesus Christ our Lord.
Amen.**

**Loving God, we thank you
that you have fed us in this Sacrament,
united us with Christ,
and given us a foretaste
of the heavenly banquet
in your eternal kingdom.
Send us out in the power of your Spirit
to live and work to your praise and glory,
in Jesus' name. Amen.**

A hymn or song may be sung.

The people are dismissed with the blessing:
Go forth in peace.
The grace of the Lord Jesus Christ,
and the love of God,
and the communion of the Holy Spirit
be with you all. **Amen.**

Either of the bracketed sections may be omitted,
depending on the occasion.

For alternative texts following this Great Thanksgiving, turn to page 58.

The Lord be with you.
And also with you.
Lift up your hearts.
We lift them to the Lord.
Let us give thanks to the Lord our God.
It is right to give our thanks and praise.

It is right, and a good and joyful thing,
always and everywhere
to give thanks to you, Father Almighty,
Creator of heaven and earth.

You brought all things into being
and called them good.
From the dust of the earth
you formed us into your image
and breathed into us the breath of life.
When we turned away, and our love failed,
your love remained steadfast.

When rain fell upon the earth
forty days and forty nights
you bore up the ark on the waters,
saved Noah and his family,
and established an everlasting covenant
with every living creature upon the earth.

When you delivered us from slavery
and made us your covenant people,
you led Moses to your mountain
for forty days and forty nights
and gave us your teachings.
You led us through the wilderness
and fed us manna for forty years
and brought us to the promised land.

When we forsook your covenant,
you led your prophet Elijah
to your mountain,
where, as he fasted
forty days and forty nights,
he heard your still small voice.

And so, with your people on earth
and all the company of heaven,
we praise your name
and join their unending hymn:

Holy, holy, holy Lord,
God of power and might,
heaven and earth are full of your glory.
Hosanna in the highest.
Blessed is he
who comes in the name of the Lord.
Hosanna in the highest.

Holy are you,
and blessed is your Son Jesus Christ.
When you gave him to save us from our sin,
your Spirit led him into the wilderness,
where he fasted
forty days and forty nights
in preparation for his ministry.
When he suffered and died on a cross
for our sin,
you raised him to life,
presented him alive to the apostles
during forty days,
and exalted him at your right hand.

By the baptism
of his suffering, death, and resurrection
you gave birth to your Church,
delivered us from slavery to sin and death,
and made with us a new covenant
by water and the Spirit.

Now, when we your people
prepare for the yearly Paschal feast
of your Son's death and resurrection,
you lead us to repentance for our sin
and the cleansing of our hearts,
that during these forty days of Lent
we may be gifted and graced
to renew the covenant you made with us
through Christ.

On the night
in which he gave himself up for us
he took bread,
gave thanks to you,
broke the bread,
gave it to his disciples, and said:
"Take, eat;
this is my body which is given for you.
Do this in remembrance of me."

When the supper was over
he took the cup,
gave thanks to you,
gave it to his disciples, and said:
"Drink from this, all of you;
this is my blood of the new covenant,
poured out for you and for many
for the forgiveness of sins.
Do this, as often as you drink it,
in remembrance of me."

And so, in remembrance
of these your mighty acts in Jesus Christ,
we offer ourselves
in praise and thanksgiving
as a holy and living sacrifice,
in union with Christ's offering for us,
as we proclaim the mystery of faith.

Christ has died,
Christ is risen,
Christ will come again.

Pour out your Holy Spirit on us,
gathered here,
and on these gifts of bread and wine.
Make them be for us
the body and blood of Christ,
that we may be for the world
the body of Christ, redeemed by his blood.

By your Spirit make us one with Christ,
one with each other,
and one in ministry to all the world,
until Christ comes in final victory
and we feast at his heavenly banquet.

Through your Son Jesus Christ,
with the Holy Spirit in your holy Church,
all honor and glory is yours,
Almighty Father, now and for ever.

Amen.

And now,
with the confidence of children of God,
let us pray:

Our Father in heaven,
hallowed be your Name,
your kingdom come,
your will be done
on earth as in heaven.
Give us today our daily bread.
Forgive us our sins
as we forgive those who sin against us.
Save us from the time of trial,
and deliver us from evil.
For the kingdom, the power, and the glory
are yours now and for ever.

The minister breaks the bread in silence,
or while saying:
Because there is one loaf,
we, who are many, are one body,
for we all partake of the one loaf.
The bread which we break
is a sharing in the body of Christ.

The minister lifts the cup in silence,
or while saying:
The cup over which we give thanks
is a sharing in the blood of Christ.

The bread and wine are given to the people,
while the congregation sings hymns.
When all have received,
the Lord's table is put in order.

The following prayer is then offered
by the minister or by all:
Eternal God,
we give you thanks for this holy mystery
in which you have given yourself to us.
Grant that we may go into the world
in the strength of your Spirit,
to give ourselves to others,
in the name of Jesus Christ our Lord.
Amen.

Here a hymn or song may be sung,
followed by the dismissal with blessing.
The grace of the Lord Jesus Christ,
and the love of God,
and the communion of the Holy Spirit
be with you all. **Amen.**

The Lord be with you.
And also with you.
Lift up your hearts.
We lift them to the Lord.
Let us give thanks to the Lord our God.
It is right to give our thanks and praise.

It is right, and a good and joyful thing,
always and everywhere
to give thanks to you, Father Almighty,
Creator of heaven and earth.

In infinite love you made us for yourself;
and when we had fallen into sin
and become subject to evil and death,
your love remained steadfast.
You bid your faithful people
cleanse their hearts
and prepare with joy
for the Paschal feast,
that, fervent in prayer and works of mercy
and renewed by your Word and sacraments
we may come to the fullness of grace
which you have prepared
for those who love you.

And so, with your people on earth
and all the company of heaven,
we praise your name
and join their unending hymn:

Holy, holy, holy Lord,
God of power and might,
heaven and earth are full of your glory.
Hosanna in the highest.
Blessed is he
who comes in the name of the Lord.
Hosanna in the highest.

Holy are you,
and blessed is your Son Jesus Christ,
whom you sent in the fullness of time
to redeem the world.
He emptied himself,
taking the form of a servant,
being born in our likeness.
He humbled himself
and became obedient unto death,
even death on a cross.

He took upon himself our sin and death
and offered himself, a perfect sacrifice
for the sin of the whole world.
By the baptism
of his suffering, death, and resurrection
you gave birth to your Church,
delivered us from slavery to sin and death,
and made with us a new covenant
by water and the Spirit.

On the night
in which he gave himself up for us
he took bread,
gave thanks to you,
broke the bread,
gave it to his disciples, and said:
"Take, eat;
this is my body which is given for you.
Do this in remembrance of me."

When the supper was over
he took the cup,
gave thanks to you,
gave it to his disciples, and said:
"Drink from this, all of you;
this is my blood of the new covenant,
poured out for you and for many
for the forgiveness of sins.
Do this, as often as you drink it,
in remembrance of me."

And so, in remembrance
of these your mighty acts in Jesus Christ,
we offer ourselves
in praise and thanksgiving
as a holy and living sacrifice,
in union with Christ's offering for us,
as we proclaim the mystery of faith.

Christ has died,
Christ is risen,
Christ will come again.

Pour out your Holy Spirit on us,
gathered here,
and on these gifts of bread and wine.
Make them be for us
the body and blood of Christ,
that we may be for the world
the body of Christ, redeemed by his blood.

By your Spirit make us one with Christ,
one with each other,
and one in ministry to all the world,
until Christ comes in final victory
and we feast at his heavenly banquet.

Through your Son Jesus Christ,
with the Holy Spirit in your holy Church,
all honor and glory is yours,
Almighty Father, now and for ever.

Amen.

And now,
with the confidence of children of God,
let us pray:

**Our Father in heaven,
hallowed be your Name,
your kingdom come,
your will be done
on earth as in heaven.
Give us today our daily bread.
Forgive us our sins
as we forgive those who sin against us.
Save us from the time of trial,
and deliver us from evil.
For the kingdom, the power, and the glory
are yours now and for ever. Amen.**

*The minister breaks the bread in silence,
or while saying:*
Because there is one loaf,
we, who are many, are one body,
for we all partake of the one loaf.
The bread which we break
is a sharing in the body of Christ.

*The minister lifts the cup in silence,
or while saying:*
The cup over which we give thanks
is a sharing in the blood of Christ.

*The bread and wine are given to the people,
with these or other words being exchanged:*
The body of Christ, given for you. **Amen.**
The blood of Christ, given for you. **Amen.**

*The congregation sings hymns
while the bread and cup are given.*

*When all have received,
the Lord's table is put in order.*

*One of the following prayers
is then offered by the minister or by all:*
**Eternal God,
we give you thanks for this holy mystery
in which you have given yourself to us.
Grant that we may go into the world
in the strength of your Spirit,
to give ourselves to others,
in the name of Jesus Christ our Lord.
Amen.**

**Loving God, we thank you
that you have fed us in this Sacrament,
united us with Christ,
and given us a foretaste
of the heavenly banquet
in your eternal kingdom.
Send us out in the power of your Spirit
to live and work to your praise and glory,
in Jesus' name. Amen.**

A hymn or song may be sung.

The people are dismissed with the blessing:
Go forth in peace.
The grace of the Lord Jesus Christ,
and the love of God,
and the communion of the Holy Spirit
be with you all. **Amen.**

Service 7 is intended for use early in Lent, such as Ash Wednesday, the First Sunday in Lent, or the first Sunday in March (if it falls within Lent).

Service 8 is intended for use later in Lent, such as Palm/Passion Sunday, the early days of Holy Week (prior to Thursday evening), or the first Sunday in April (if it falls within Lent).

For alternative texts following this Great Thanksgiving, turn to page 58.

The Lord be with you.
And also with you.
Lift up your hearts.
We lift them to the Lord.
Let us give thanks to the Lord our God.
It is right to give our thanks and praise.

It is right, and a good and joyful thing,
always and everywhere
to give thanks to you, Father Almighty,
Creator of heaven and earth.

From the earth you bring forth bread
and create the fruit of the vine.
You formed us in your image,
delivered us from captivity,
and made covenant to be our sovereign God.
You fed us manna in the wilderness,
and gave grapes
to evidence the promised land.

And so, with your people on earth
and all the company of heaven,
we praise your name
and join their unending hymn:

Holy, holy, holy Lord,
God of power and might,
heaven and earth are full of your glory.
Hosanna in the highest.
Blessed is he
who comes in the name of the Lord.
Hosanna in the highest.

Holy are you,
and blessed is your Son Jesus Christ.
When we had turned aside from your way
and abused your gifts,
you gave us in him your crowning gift.
Emptying himself,
that our joy might be full,
he fed the hungry, healed the sick,
ate with the scorned and forgotten,
washed his disciples' feet,
and gave a holy meal
as the pledge of his abiding presence.

By the baptism
of his suffering, death, and resurrection
you gave birth to your Church,
delivered us from slavery to sin and death,
and made with us a new covenant
by water and the Spirit.

On the night
in which he gave himself up for us
he took bread,
gave thanks to you,
broke the bread,
gave it to his disciples, and said:
"Take, eat;
this is my body which is given for you.
Do this in remembrance of me."

When the supper was over
he took the cup,
gave thanks to you,
gave it to his disciples, and said:
"Drink from this, all of you;
this is my blood of the new covenant,
poured out for you and for many
for the forgiveness of sins.
Do this, as often as you drink it,
in remembrance of me."

And so, in remembrance
of these your mighty acts in Jesus Christ,
we offer ourselves
in praise and thanksgiving
as a holy and living sacrifice,
in union with Christ's offering for us,
as we proclaim the mystery of faith.

Christ has died,
Christ is risen,
Christ will come again.

Pour out your holy Spirit on us,
gathered here,
and on these gifts of bread and wine.
Make them be for us
the body and blood of Christ,
that we may be for the world
the body of Christ, redeemed by his blood.

By your Spirit make us one with Christ,
one with each other,
and one in ministry to all the world,
until Christ comes in final victory
and we feast at his heavenly banquet.

Through your Son Jesus Christ,
with the Holy Spirit in your holy Church,
all honor and glory is yours,
Almighty Father, now and for ever.

Amen.

And now,
with the confidence of children of God,
let us pray:

**Our Father in heaven,
hallowed be your Name,
your kingdom come,
your will be done
on earth as in heaven.
Give us today our daily bread.
Forgive us our sins
as we forgive those who sin against us.
Save us from the time of trial,
and deliver us from evil.
For the kingdom, the power, and the glory
are yours now and for ever. Amen.**

*The minister breaks the bread in silence,
or while saying:*
Because there is one loaf,
we, who are many, are one body,
for we all partake of the one loaf.
The bread which we break
is a sharing in the body of Christ.

*The minister lifts the cup in silence,
or while saying:*
The cup over which we give thanks
is a sharing in the blood of Christ.

*The bread and wine are given to the people,
with these or other words being exchanged:*
The body of Christ, given for you. **Amen.**
The blood of Christ, given for you. **Amen.**

*The congregation sings hymns
while the bread and cup are given.*

*When all have received,
the Lord's table is put in order.*

*One of the following prayers
is then offered by the minister or by all:*
**Eternal God,
we give you thanks for this holy mystery
in which you have given yourself to us.
Grant that we may go into the world
in the strength of your Spirit,
to give ourselves to others,
in the name of Jesus Christ our Lord.
Amen.**

**Loving God, we thank you
that you have fed us in this Sacrament,
united us with Christ,
and given us a foretaste
of the heavenly banquet
in your eternal kingdom.
Send us out in the power of your Spirit
to live and work to your praise and glory,
in Jesus' name. Amen.**

A hymn or song may be sung.

The people are dismissed with the blessing:
Go forth in peace.
The grace of the Lord Jesus Christ,
and the love of God,
and the communion of the Holy Spirit
be with you all.

Amen.

For alternative texts following this Great Thanksgiving, turn to page 58.

The Lord be with you.
And also with you.
Lift up your hearts.
We lift them to the Lord.
Let us give thanks to the Lord our God.
It is right to give our thanks and praise.

It is right, and a good and joyful thing,
always and everywhere
to give thanks to you, Father Almighty,
Creator of heaven and earth.

You formed us in your image
and breathed into us the breath of life.
When we turned away, and our love failed,
your love remained steadfast.
You delivered us from captivity,
made covenant to be our sovereign God,
brought us to a land
flowing with milk and honey,
and set before us the way of life.

And so, with your people on earth
and all the company of heaven,
we praise your name
and join their unending hymn:

Holy, holy, holy Lord,
God of power and might,
heaven and earth are full of your glory.
Hosanna in the highest.
Blessed is he
who comes in the name of the Lord.
Hosanna in the highest.

Holy are you,
and blessed is your Son Jesus Christ.
By the baptism
of his suffering, death, and resurrection
you gave birth to your Church,
delivered us from slavery to sin and death,
and made with us a new covenant
by water and the Spirit.

By your great mercy
we have been born anew to a living hope
through the resurrection of your Son
from the dead,

and to an inheritance which is
imperishable, undefiled, and unfading.
Once we were no people,
but now we are your people,
declaring your wonderful deeds in Christ,
who called us out of darkness
into his marvelous light.

When the Lord Jesus ascended,
he promised to be with us always,
in the power of your Word and Holy Spirit.

On the night
in which he gave himself up for us
he took bread,
gave thanks to you,
broke the bread,
gave it to his disciples, and said:
"Take, eat;
this is my body which is given for you.
Do this in remembrance of me."

When the supper was over
he took the cup,
gave thanks to you,
gave it to his disciples, and said:
"Drink from this, all of you;
this is my blood of the new covenant,
poured out for you and for many
for the forgiveness of sins.
Do this, as often as you drink it,
in remembrance of me."

On the day you raised him from the dead
he was recognized by his disciples
in the breaking of the bread,
and in the power of your Holy Spirit
your Church has continued
in the breaking of bread
and the sharing of the cup.

And so, in remembrance
of these your mighty acts in Jesus Christ,
we offer ourselves
in praise and thanksgiving
as a holy and living sacrifice.
in union with Christ's offering for us,
as we proclaim the mystery of faith.

Christ has died,
Christ is risen,
Christ will come again.

Pour out your Holy Spirit on us,
gathered here,
and on these gifts of bread and wine.
Make them be for us
the body and blood of Christ,
that we may be for the world
the body of Christ, redeemed by his blood.

By your Spirit make us one with Christ,
one with each other,
and one in ministry to all the world,
until Christ comes in final victory
and we feast at his heavenly banquet.

Through your Son Jesus Christ,
with the Holy Spirit in your holy Church,
all honor and glory is yours,
Almighty Father, now and for ever.

Amen.

And now,
with the confidence of children of God,
let us pray:

Our Father in heaven,
hallowed be your Name,
your kingdom come,
your will be done
on earth as in heaven.
Give us today our daily bread.
Forgive us our sins
as we forgive those who sin against us.
Save us from the time of trial,
and deliver us from evil.
For the kingdom, the power, and the glory
are yours now and for ever. Amen.

The minister breaks the bread in silence,
or while saying:
Because there is one loaf,
we, who are many, are one body,
for we all partake of the one loaf.
The bread which we break
is a sharing in the body of Christ.

The minister lifts the cup in silence,
or while saying:
The cup over which we give thanks
is a sharing in the blood of Christ.

The bread and wine are given to the people,
with these or other words being exchanged:
The body of Christ, given for you. **Amen.**
The blood of Christ, given for you. **Amen.**

The congregation sings hymns
while the bread and cup are given.

When all have received,
the Lord's table is put in order.

The following prayer is then offered
by the minister or by all:
Loving God, we thank you
that you have fed us in this Sacrament,
united us with Christ,
and given us a foretaste
of the heavenly banquet
in your eternal kingdom.
Send us out in the power of your Spirit
to live and work to your praise and glory,
in Jesus' name. Amen.

A hymn or song may be sung.

The people are dismissed with the blessing:
Go forth in peace.
The grace of the Lord Jesus Christ,
and the love of God,
and the communion of the Holy Spirit
be with you all.

Amen.

Service 10 is intended for use at the Easter Vigil, Easter Day, Ascension, or at any time in the Easter Season prior to Pentecost.

For alternative texts following this Great Thanksgiving, turn to page 58.

The Lord be with you.
And also with you.
Lift up your hearts.
We lift them to the Lord.
Let us give thanks to the Lord our God.
It is right to give our thanks and praise.

It is right, and a good and joyful thing,
always and everywhere
to give thanks to you, Father Almighty,
Creator of heaven and earth.

In the beginning your Spirit
moved over the face of the waters.
You formed us in your image
and breathed into us the breath of life.
When we turned away, and our love failed,
your love remained steadfast.
Your Spirit
came upon prophets and teachers,
anointing them to speak your Word.

And so, with your people on earth
and all the company of heaven,
we praise your name
and join their unending hymn:

Holy, holy, holy Lord,
God of power and might,
heaven and earth are full of your glory.
Hosanna in the highest.
Blessed is he
who comes in the name of the Lord.
Hosanna in the highest.

Holy are you,
and blessed is your Son Jesus Christ.
At his baptism in the Jordan
your Spirit descended upon him
and declared him your beloved Son.
With your Spirit upon him
he turned away the temptations of sin.
Your Spirit anointed him
to preach good news to the poor,
to proclaim release to the captives
and recovering of sight to the blind,
to set at liberty those who are oppressed,

and to announce that the time had come
when you would save your people.
He healed the sick, fed the hungry,
and ate with sinners.

By the baptism
of his suffering, death, and resurrection
you gave birth to your Church,
delivered us from slavery to sin and death,
and made with us a new covenant
by water and the Spirit.
When the Lord Jesus ascended,
he promised to be with us always,
baptizing us
with the Holy Spirit and with fire,
as on the Day of Pentecost.

On the night
in which he gave himself up for us
he took bread,
gave thanks to you,
broke the bread,
gave it to his disciples, and said:
"Take, eat;
this is my body which is given for you.
Do this in remembrance of me."

When the supper was over
he took the cup,
gave thanks to you,
gave it to his disciples, and said:
"Drink from this, all of you;
this is my blood of the new covenant,
poured out for you and for many
for the forgiveness of sins.
Do this, as often as you drink it,
in remembrance of me."

On the day you raised him from the dead
he was recognized by his disciples
in the breaking of the bread,
and in the power of your Holy Spirit
your Church has continued
in the breaking of bread
and the sharing of the cup.

And so, in remembrance
of these your mighty acts in Jesus Christ,

we offer ourselves
in praise and thanksgiving
as a holy and living sacrifice,
in union with Christ's offering for us,
as we proclaim the mystery of faith.

**Christ has died,
Christ is risen,
Christ will come again.**

Pour out your Holy Spirit on us,
gathered here,
and on these gifts of bread and wine.
Make them be for us
the body and blood of Christ,
that we may be for the world
the body of Christ, redeemed by his blood.

By your Spirit make us one with Christ,
one with each other,
and one in ministry to all the world,
until Christ comes in final victory
and we feast at his heavenly banquet.

Through your Son Jesus Christ,
with the Holy Spirit in your holy Church,
all honor and glory is yours,
Almighty Father, now and for ever.

Amen.

And now,
with the confidence of children of God,
let us pray:

**Our Father in heaven,
hallowed be your Name,
your kingdom come,
your will be done
on earth as in heaven.
Give us today our daily bread.
Forgive us our sins
as we forgive those who sin against us.
Save us from the time of trial,
and deliver us from evil.
For the kingdom, the power, and the glory
are yours now and for ever. Amen.**

*The minister breaks the bread in silence,
or while saying:*
Because there is one loaf,
we, who are many, are one body,
for we all partake of the one loaf.
The bread which we break
is a sharing in the body of Christ.

*The minister lifts the cup in silence,
or while saying:*
The cup over which we give thanks
is a sharing in the blood of Christ.

*The bread and wine are given to the people,
with these or other words being exchanged:*
The body of Christ, given for you. **Amen.**
The blood of Christ, given for you. **Amen.**

*The congregation sings hymns
while the bread and cup are given.*

*When all have received,
the Lord's table is put in order.*

*The following prayer is then offered
by the minister or by all:*
**Eternal God,
we give you thanks for this holy mystery
in which you have given yourself to us.
Grant that we may go into the world
in the strength of your Spirit,
to give ourselves to others,
in the name of Jesus Christ our Lord.
Amen.**

A hymn or song may be sung.

The people are dismissed with the blessing:
Go forth in peace.
The grace of the Lord Jesus Christ,
and the love of God,
and the communion of the Holy Spirit
be with you all.

Amen.

For alternate texts following this Great Thanksgiving, turn to page 58.

The Lord be with you.
And also with you.
Lift up your hearts.
We lift them to the Lord.
Let us give thanks to the Lord our God.
It is right to give our thanks and praise.

It is right, and a good and joyful thing,
always and everywhere
to give thanks to you, Father Almighty,
Creator of heaven and earth.

You formed us in your image
and breathed into us the breath of life.
When we turned away, and our love failed,
your love remained steadfast.
You delivered us from captivity,
made covenant to be our sovereign God,
and spoke to us through your prophets,
who looked for that day
when justice shall roll down like waters
and righteousness
like an ever-flowing stream,
when nation shall not lift up sword
against nation,
neither shall they learn war any more.

And so, with your people on earth
and all the company of heaven,
we praise your name
and join their unending hymn:

Holy, holy, holy Lord,
God of power and might,
heaven and earth are full of your glory.
Hosanna in the highest.
Blessed is he
who comes in the name of the Lord.
Hosanna in the highest.

Holy are you,
and blessed is your Son Jesus Christ.
Your Spirit anointed him
to preach good news to the poor,
to proclaim release to the captives
and recovering of sight to the blind,
to set at liberty those who are oppressed,
and to announce that the time had come
when you would save your people.

He healed the sick, fed the hungry,
and ate with sinners.

By the baptism
of his suffering, death, and resurrection
you gave birth to your Church,
delivered us from slavery to sin and death,
and made with us a new covenant
by water and the Spirit.
At his ascension you exalted him
to sit and reign with you at your right hand.

On the night
in which he gave himself up for us
he took bread,
gave it to his disciples, and said:
"Take, eat;
this is my body which is given for you.
Do this in remembrance of me."

When the supper was over
he took the cup,
gave thanks to you,
gave it to his disciples, and said:
"Drink from this, all of you;
this is my blood of the new covenant,
poured out for you and for many
for the forgiveness of sins.
Do this, as often as you drink it,
in remembrance of me."

And so, in remembrance
of these your mighty acts in Jesus Christ,
we offer ourselves
in praise and thanksgiving
as a holy and living sacrifice,
in union with Christ's offering for us,
as we proclaim the mystery of faith.

Christ has died,
Christ is risen,
Christ will come again.

Pour out your Holy Spirit on us,
gathered here,
and on these gifts of bread and wine.
Make them be for us
the body and blood of Christ,
that we may be for the world
the body of Christ, redeemed by his blood.

CHRIST THE KING

By your Spirit make us one with Christ,
one with each other,
and one in ministry to all the world,
until Christ comes in final victory
and we feast at his heavenly banquet.

Through your Son Jesus Christ,
with the Holy Spirit in your holy Church,
all honor and glory is yours,
Almighty Father, now and for ever.

Amen.

And now,
with the confidence of children of God,
let us pray:

**Our Father in heaven,
hallowed be your Name,
your kingdom come,
your will be done
on earth as in heaven.
Give us today our daily bread.
Forgive us our sins
as we forgive those who sin against us.
Save us from the time of trial,
and deliver us from evil.
For the kingdom, the power, and the glory
are yours now and for ever. Amen.**

*The minister breaks the bread in silence,
or while saying:*
Because there is one loaf,
we, who are many, are one body,
for we all partake of the one loaf.
The bread which we break
is a sharing in the body of Christ.

*The minister lifts the cup in silence,
or while saying:*
The cup over which we give thanks
is a sharing in the blood of Christ.

*The bread and wine are given to the people,
with these or other words being exchanged:*
The body of Christ, given for you. **Amen.**
The blood of Christ, given for you. **Amen.**

*The congregation sings hymns
while the bread and cup are given.*

*When all have received,
the Lord's table is put in order.*

*One of the following prayers is then offered
by the minister or by all:*
**Eternal God,
we give you thanks for this holy mystery
in which you have given yourself to us.
Grant that we may go into the world
in the strength of your Spirit,
to give ourselves to others,
in the name of Jesus Christ our Lord.
Amen.**

**Loving God, we thank you
that you have fed us in this Sacrament,
united us with Christ,
and given us a foretaste
of the heavenly banquet
in your eternal kingdom.
Send us out in the power of your Spirit
to live and work to your praise and glory,
in Jesus' name. Amen.**

A hymn or song may be sung.

The people are dismissed with the blessing:
Go forth in peace.
The grace of the Lord Jesus Christ,
and the love of God,
and the communion of the Holy Spirit
be with you all.

Amen.

Service 12 is intended for use on the Last Sunday after Pentecost (Christ the King) or on any Sunday after Pentecost when the coming of the Kingdom of God is emphasized or Kingdomtide is observed.

For alternative texts following this Great Thanksgiving, turn to page 58.

The Lord be with you.
And also with you.
Lift up your hearts.
We lift them to the Lord.
Let us give thanks to the Lord our God.
It is right to give our thanks and praise.

It is right, and a good and joyful thing,
always and everywhere
to give thanks to you, Father Almighty,
Creator of heaven and earth.

Blessed are you,
God of creation and all beginnings,
God of Abraham and Sarah,
God of Miriam and Moses,
God of Joshua and Deborah,
God of Ruth and David,
God of the priests and the prophets,
God of Mary and Joseph,
God of the apostles and the martyrs,
God of our mothers and our fathers,
God of our children to all generations.
And so, with your people on earth
and all the company of heaven,
we praise your name
and join their unending hymn:

Holy, holy, holy Lord,
God of power and might,
heaven and earth are full of your glory.
Hosanna in the highest.
Blessed is he
who comes in the name of the Lord.
Hosanna in the highest.

Holy are you,
and blessed is your Son Jesus Christ.
By the baptism
of his suffering, death, and resurrection
you gave birth to your Church,
delivered us from slavery to sin and death,
and made with us a new covenant
by water and the Spirit.

On the night
in which he gave himself up for us
he took bread,
gave thanks to you,
broke the bread,
gave it to his disciples, and said:
"Take, eat;
this is my body which is given for you.
Do this in remembrance of me."

When the supper was over
he took the cup,
gave thanks to you,
gave it to his disciples, and said:
"Drink from this, all of you;
this is my blood of the new covenant,
poured out for you and for many
for the forgiveness of sins.
Do this, as often as you drink it,
in remembrance of me."

And so, in remembrance
of these your mighty acts in Jesus Christ,
we offer ourselves
in praise and thanksgiving
as a holy and living sacrifice,
in union with Christ's offering for us,
as we proclaim the mystery of faith.

Christ has died,
Christ is risen,
Christ will come again.

Pour out your Holy Spirit on us,
gathered here,
and on these gifts of bread and wine.
Make them be for us
the body and blood of Christ,
that we may be for the world
the body of Christ, redeemed by his blood.

Renew our communion with all your saints,
especially those whom we name before you,
(*optional names or*) in our hearts.
Since we are surrounded
by so great a cloud of witnesses,
strengthen us to run with perseverance
the race that is set before us,
looking to Jesus,
the pioneer and perfecter of our faith.

By your Spirit make us one with Christ,
one with each other,
and one in ministry to all the world,
until Christ comes in final victory
and we feast at his heavenly banquet.

Through your Son Jesus Christ,
with the Holy Spirit in your holy Church,
all honor and glory is yours,
Almighty Father, now and for ever.

Amen.

And now,
with the confidence of children of God,
let us pray:

**Our Father in heaven,
hallowed be your Name,
your kingdom come,
your will be done
on earth as in heaven.
Give us today our daily bread.
Forgive us our sins
as we forgive those who sin against us.
Save us from the time of trial,
and deliver us from evil.
For the kingdom, the power, and the glory
are yours now and for ever. Amen.**

*The minister breaks the bread in silence,
or while saying:*
Because there is one loaf,
we, who are many, are one body,
for we all partake of the one loaf.
The bread which we break
is a sharing in the body of Christ.

*The minister lifts the cup in silence,
or while saying:*
The cup over which we give thanks
is a sharing in the blood of Christ.

*The bread and wine are given to the people,
with these or other words being exchanged:*
The body of Christ, given for you. **Amen.**
The blood of Christ, given for you. **Amen.**

*The congregation sings hymns
while the bread and cup are given.*

*When all have received,
the Lord's table is put in order.*

*One of the following prayers
is then offered by the minister or
by all:*
**Eternal God,
we give you thanks for this holy mystery
in which you have given yourself to us.
Grant that we may go into the world
in the strength of your Spirit,
to give ourselves to others,
in the name of Jesus Christ our Lord.
Amen.**

**Loving God, we thank you
that you have fed us in this Sacrament,
united us with Christ,
and given us a foretaste
of the heavenly banquet
in your eternal kingdom.
Send us out in the power of your Spirit
to live and work to your praise and glory,
in Jesus' name. Amen.**

A hymn or song may be sung.

The people are dismissed with the blessing:
Go forth in peace.
The grace of the Lord Jesus Christ,
and the love of God,
and the communion of the Holy Spirit
be with you all.

Amen.

For alternative texts following this Great Thanksgiving, turn to page 58.

The Lord be with you.
And also with you.
Lift up your hearts.
We lift them to the Lord.
Let us give thanks to the Lord our God.
It is right to give our thanks and praise.

It is right, and a good and joyful thing,
always and everywhere
to give thanks to you, Father Almighty,
Creator of heaven and earth.

By your appointment
the seasons come and go.
You bring forth bread from the earth
and create the fruit of the vine.
You have made us in your image
and given us dominion over the world.
Earth has yielded its treasure,
and from your hand
we have received blessing on blessing.

And so, with your people on earth
and all the company of heaven,
we praise your name
and join their unending hymn:

Holy, holy, holy Lord,
God of power and might,
heaven and earth are full of your glory.
Hosanna in the highest.
Blessed is he
who comes in the name of the Lord.
Hosanna in the highest.

Holy are you,
and blessed is your Son Jesus Christ.
Though he was rich,
yet for our sake he became poor.
When hungry and tempted,
he refused to make bread for himself
that he might be the bread of life
for others.
When the multitudes were hungry,
he fed them.
He broke bread with the outcast
but drove the greedy out of the Temple.

By the baptism
of his suffering, death, and resurrection
you gave birth to your Church,
delivered us from slavery to sin and death,
and made with us a new covenant
by water and the Spirit.

On the night
in which he gave himself up for us
he took bread,
gave thanks to you,
broke the bread,
gave it to his disciples, and said:
"Take, eat;
this is my body which is given for you.
Do this in remembrance of me."

When the supper was over
he took the cup,
gave thanks to you,
gave it to his disciples, and said:
"Drink from this, all of you;
this is my blood of the new covenant,
poured out for you and for many
for the forgiveness of sins.
Do this, as often as you drink it,
in remembrance of me."

And so, in remembrance
of these your mighty acts in Jesus Christ,
we offer ourselves
in praise and thanksgiving
as a holy and living sacrifice,
in union with Christ's offering for us,
as we proclaim the mystery of faith.

Christ has died,
Christ is risen,
Christ will come again.

Pour out your Holy Spirit on us,
gathered here,
and on these gifts of bread and wine.
Make them be for us
the body and blood of Christ,
that we may be for the world
the body of Christ, redeemed by his blood.

By your Spirit make us one with Christ,
one with each other,
and one in ministry to all the world,
until Christ comes in final victory
and we feast at his heavenly banquet.

Through your Son Jesus Christ,
with the Holy Spirit in your holy Church,
all honor and glory is yours,
Almighty Father, now and for ever.

Amen.

And now,
with the confidence of children of God,
let us pray:

**Our Father in heaven,
hallowed be your Name,
your kingdom come,
your will be done
on earth as in heaven.
Give us today our daily bread.
Forgive us our sins
as we forgive those who sin against us.
Save us from the time of trial,
and deliver us from evil.
For the kingdom, the power, and the glory
are yours now and for ever. Amen.**

*The minister breaks the bread in silence,
or while saying:*
Because there is one loaf,
we, who are many, are one body,
for we all partake of the one loaf.
The bread which we break
is a sharing in the body of Christ.

*The minister lifts the cup in silence,
or while saying:*
The cup over which we give thanks
is a sharing in the blood of Christ.

*The bread and wine are given to the people,
with these or other words being exchanged:*
The body of Christ, given for you. **Amen.**
The blood of Christ, given for you. **Amen.**

*The congregation sings hymns,
while the bread and cup are given.*

*When all have received,
the Lord's table is put in order.*

*One of the following prayers is then offered
by the minister or by all:*
**Eternal God,
we give you thanks for this holy mystery
in which you have given yourself to us.
Grant that we may go into the world
in the strength of your Spirit,
to give ourselves to others,
in the name of Jesus Christ our Lord.
Amen.**

**Loving God, we thank you
that you have fed us in this Sacrament,
united us with Christ,
and given us a foretaste
of the heavenly banquet
in your eternal kingdom.
Send us out in the power of your Spirit
to live and work to your praise and glory,
in Jesus' name. Amen.**

A hymn or song may be sung.

The people are dismissed with the blessing:
Go forth in peace.
The grace of the Lord Jesus Christ,
and the love of God,
and the communion of the Holy Spirit
be with you all.

Amen.

Service 14 is intended for use on Thanksgiving or any other occasion when the gift of food is celebrated.

For alternative texts following this Great Thanksgiving, turn to page 58.

The Lord be with you.
And also with you.
Lift up your hearts.
We lift them to the Lord.
Let us give thanks to the Lord our God.
It is right to give our thanks and praise.

It is right, and a good and joyful thing,
always and everywhere
to give thanks to you, Father Almighty,
Creator of heaven and earth.

You formed us in your image,
male and female you created us.
You gave us the gift of marriage,
that we might fulfill one another.

And so, with your people on earth
and all the company of heaven
we praise your name
and join their unending hymn:

Holy, holy, holy Lord,
God of power and might,
heaven and earth are full of your glory.
Hosanna in the highest.
Blessed is he
who comes in the name of the Lord.
Hosanna in the highest.

Holy are you,
and blessed is your Son Jesus Christ.
By the baptism
of his suffering, death, and resurrection
you gave birth to your Church,
delivered us from slavery to sin and death,
and made with us a new covenant
by water and the Spirit,
from which flows the covenant love
of husband and wife.

On the night
in which he gave himself up for us
he took bread,
gave thanks to you,
broke the bread,
gave it to his disciples, and said:

"Take, eat;
this is my body which is given for you.
Do this in remembrance of me."

When the supper was over
he took the cup,
gave thanks to you,
gave it to his disciples, and said:
"Drink from this, all of you;
this is my blood of the new covenant,
poured out for you and for many
for the remission of sins.
Do this, as often as you drink it,
in remembrance of me."

And so, in remembrance
of these your mighty acts in Jesus Christ,
we offer ourselves
in praise and thanksgiving
as a holy and living sacrifice,
in union with Christ's offering for us,
as we proclaim the mystery of faith.

Christ has died,
Christ is risen,
Christ will come again.

Pour out your Holy Spirit on us,
gathered here,
and on these gifts of bread and wine.
Make them be for us
the body and blood of Christ,
that we may be for the world
the body of Christ, redeemed by his blood.

By the same Spirit bless *Name* and *Name*,
that their love for each other
may reflect the love of Christ for us
and grow from strength to strength
as they faithfully serve you in the world.
Finally, by your grace,
bring them and all of us to that table
where your saints feast forever
in your heavenly home.

Through your Son Jesus Christ,
with the Holy Spirit in your holy Church,

all honor and glory is yours,
Almighty Father, now and for ever.

Amen.

And now,
with the confidence of children of God,
let us pray:

**Our Father in heaven,
hallowed be your Name,
your kingdom come,
your will be done
on earth as in heaven.
Give us today our daily bread.
Forgive us our sins
as we forgive those who sin against us.
Save us from the time of trial,
and deliver us from evil.
For the kingdom, the power, and the glory
are yours now and for ever. Amen.**

*The minister breaks the bread in silence,
or while saying:*
Because there is one loaf,
we, who are many, are one body,
for we all partake of the one loaf.
The bread which we break
is a sharing in the body of Christ.

*The minister lifts the cup in silence,
or while saying:*
The cup over which we give thanks
is a sharing in the blood of Christ.

*The bread and wine are given to the people,
with these or other words being exchanged:*
The body of Christ, given for you. **Amen.**
The blood of Christ, given for you. **Amen.**

Here may be a hymn or psalm.

The people are dismissed with the blessing:
God the Eternal
keep you in love with each other,
so that the peace of Christ
may abide in your home.
Go to serve God and your neighbor
in all that you do.
Bear witness to the love of God
in this world
so that those to whom love is a stranger
will find in you generous friends.
The grace of the Lord Jesus Christ,
and the love of God,
and the communion of the Holy Spirit
be with you all.

Amen.

Service 15 is intended for use with "A Service of Christian Marriage" in *The Book of Services* (see Sources, p. 60).

The Lord be with you.
And also with you.
Lift up your hearts.
We lift them to the Lord.
Let us give thanks to the Lord our God.
It is right to give our thanks and praise.

It is right,
that we should always and everywhere
give thanks to you, Father Almighty,
Creator of heaven and earth,
through Jesus Christ our Lord,
who rose victorious from the dead
and comforts us
with the blessed hope of everlasting life.

And so, with your people on earth
and all the company of heaven,
we praise your name
and join their unending hymn:

Holy, holy, holy Lord,
God of power and might,
heaven and earth are full of your glory.
Hosanna in the highest.
Blessed is he
who comes in the name of the Lord.
Hosanna in the highest.

Holy are you,
and blessed is your Son Jesus Christ.
By the baptism
of his suffering, death, and resurrection
you gave birth to your Church,
delivered us from slavery to sin and death,
and made with us a new covenant,
by water and the Spirit.
When the Lord Jesus ascended
he promised to be with us always
in the power of your Word and Holy Spirit.

On the night
in which he gave himself up for us
he took bread,
gave it to his disciples, and said:
"Take, eat;
this is my body which is given to you.
Do this in remembrance of me."

When the supper was over
he took the cup,
gave thanks to you,
gave it to his disciples, and said:
"Drink from this, all of you;
this is my blood of the new covenant,
poured out for you and for many
for the forgiveness of sins.
Do this, as often as you drink it,
in remembrance of me."

And so, in remembrance
of these your mighty acts in Jesus Christ,
we offer ourselves
in praise and thanksgiving
as a holy and living sacrifice,
in union with Christ's offering for us,
as we proclaim the mystery of faith.

Christ has died,
Christ is risen,
Christ will come again.

Pour out your Holy Spirit on us,
gathered here,
and on these gifts of bread and wine.
Make them be for us
the body and blood of Christ,
that we may be for the world
the body of Christ, redeemed by his blood.

By your Spirit make us one with Christ,
one with each other,
and one in communion with all your saints,
especially *Name*
and all those most dear to us.
Finally, by your grace,
bring them and all of us to that table
where your saints feast forever
in your heavenly home.

Through your Son Jesus Christ,
with the Holy Spirit in your holy Church,
all honor and glory is yours,
Almighty Father, now and for ever.

Amen.

And now,
with the confidence of children of God,
let us pray:

**Our Father in heaven,
hallowed be your Name,
your kingdom come,
your will be done
on earth as in heaven.
Give us today our daily bread.
Forgive us our sins
as we forgive those who sin against us.
Save us from the time of trial,
and deliver us from evil.
For the kingdom, the power, and the glory
are yours now and for ever. Amen.**

*The minister breaks the bread in silence,
or while saying:*
Because there is one loaf,
we, who are many, are one body,
for we all partake of the one loaf.
The bread which we break
is a sharing in the body of Christ.

*The minister lifts the cup in silence,
or while saying:*
The cup over which we give thanks
is a sharing in the blood of Christ.

*The bread and wine are given to the people,
with these or other words being exchanged:*
The body of Christ, given for you. **Amen.**
The blood of Christ, given for you. **Amen.**

*During the giving of the bread and wine
hymns or songs of praise may be sung.*

*When all have received,
the Lord's table is put in order.*

*The people are dismissed
with one or more
of the following blessings:*

Now may the God of Peace
who brought again from the dead
our Lord Jesus,
the great Shepherd of the sheep,

by the blood of the eternal covenant,
equip you with everything good
that you may do his will,
working in you
that which is pleasing in his sight,
through Jesus Christ;
to whom be glory for ever and ever.
Amen.

The peace of God
which passes all understanding
keep your hearts and minds
in the knowledge and love of God,
and of his Son Jesus Christ our Lord.
And the blessing of God Almighty,
the Father, Son, and Holy Spirit,
be among you and remain with you always.
Amen.

Now may the Father
from whom every family
in heaven and on earth
is named,
according to the riches of his glory,
grant you to be strengthened with might
through his Spirit in your inner being,
that Christ may dwell in your hearts
through faith;
that you,
being rooted and grounded in love,
may be able to comprehend
with all the saints
what is the breadth and length
and height and depth,
and to know the love of Christ
which surpasses knowledge,
that you may be filled
with all the fullness of God.
Amen.

Now to the One
who by the power at work within us
is able to do far more abundantly
than all that we ask or think,
to this God be glory in the Church
and in Christ Jesus
to all generations, for ever and ever.
Amen.

The Lord be with you.
And also with you.
Lift up your hearts.
We lift them to the Lord.
Let us give thanks to the Lord our God.
It is right to give our thanks and praise.

Blessed are you, Sovereign of the Ages,
whose strong and loving arms
encompass the universe,
for with your eternal Word and Holy Spirit
you are for ever one God.
Through your Word you created all things
and called them good,
and in you
we live and move and have our being.

When we fell into sin
you did not desert us.
You made covenant
with your people Israel
and spoke through teachers and prophets.
In Jesus Christ
your Word became flesh
and dwelt among us,
full of grace and truth.
And so, with your people on earth
and all the company of heaven,
we praise your name
and join their unending hymn:

Holy, holy, holy Lord,
God of power and might,
heaven and earth are full of your glory.
Hosanna in the highest.
Blessed is the One
who comes in the name of the Lord.
Hosanna in the highest.

Holy are you,
and blessed is Jesus Christ,
who called you Abba, Father.
As a mother tenderly gathers her children,
you embraced a people as your own
and filled them with longing
for a peace that would last
and for a justice that would never fail.

In Jesus' suffering and death
you took upon yourself our sin and death,
offered a perfect sacrifice
for the sin of the whole world,
and destroyed the power of sin and death.
You raised from the dead this same Jesus,
who now reigns with you in glory,
and poured upon us your Holy Spirit,
making us
the people of your new covenant.

On the night before meeting with death
Jesus took bread,
gave thanks to you,
broke the bread,
gave it to the disciples, and said:
"Take, eat;
this is my body which is given for you.
Do this in remembrance of me."

When the supper was over
Jesus took the cup,
gave thanks to you,
gave it to the disciples, and said:
"Drink from this, all of you;
this is my blood of the new covenant,
poured out for you and for many
for the forgiveness of sins.
Do this, as often as you drink it,
in remembrance of me."

And so, in remembrance
of these your mighty acts in Jesus Christ,
we offer ourselves
in praise and thanksgiving
as a holy and living sacrifice,
in union with Christ's offering for us,
as we proclaim the mystery of faith.

Christ has died,
Christ is risen,
Christ will come again.

Pour out your Holy Spirit on us,
gathered here,
and on these gifts of bread and wine.

Make them be for us
the body and blood of Christ,
that we may be for the world
the body of Christ,
redeemed by Christ's blood.

As the grain and grapes
once dispersed in the fields
are now united on this table
in bread and wine,
so may we and all your people
be gathered from every time and place
into the unity of your eternal household
and feast at your table for ever.

Through Christ, with Christ, in Christ,
in the unity of the Holy Spirit,
all honor and glory is yours,
Almighty God, now and for ever.

Amen.

And now,
with the confidence of children of God,
let us pray:

**Our Father in heaven,
hallowed be your Name,
your kingdom come,
your will be done
on earth as in heaven.
Give us today our daily bread.
Forgive us our sins
as we forgive those who sin against us.
Save us from the time of trial,
and deliver us from evil.
For the kingdom, the power, and the glory
are yours now and for ever. Amen.**

*The minister breaks the bread in silence,
or while saying:*
Because there is one loaf,
we, who are many, are one body,
for we all partake of the one loaf.
The bread which we break
is a sharing in the body of Christ.

*The minister lifts the cup in silence,
or while saying:*
The cup over which we give thanks
is a sharing in the blood of Christ.

*The bread and wine are given to the people,
with these or other words being exchanged:*
The body of Christ, given for you. **Amen.**
The blood of Christ, given for you. **Amen.**

*The congregation sings hymns
while the bread and cup are given.*

*When all have received,
the Lord's table is put in order.*

*The following prayer is then offered
by the minister or by all:*
**Eternal God,
we give you thanks for this holy mystery
in which you have given yourself to us.
Grant that we may go into the world
in the strength of your Spirit,
to give ourselves to others,
in the name of Jesus Christ our Lord.
Amen.**

A hymn or song may be sung.

The people are dismissed with the blessing:
Go forth in peace.
The grace the Lord of Jesus Christ,
and the love of God,
and the communion of the Holy Spirit
be with you all.

Amen.

The sentence beginning, "As the grain," is adapted
from the *Didache (The Teaching of the Twelve Apostles),*
which dates from the late first or early second
century. See page 57.

For alternative texts following this Great Thanksgiving, turn to page 58.

The Lord be with you.
And also with you.
Lift up your hearts.
We lift them to the Lord.
Let us give thanks to the Lord our God.
It is right to give our thanks and praise.

Blessed are you, O God,
who with your Word and Holy Spirit
created all things and called them good.

And so, with your people on earth
and all the company of heaven,
we praise your name
and join their unending hymn:

Holy, holy, holy Lord,
God of power and might,
heaven and earth are full of your glory.
Hosanna in the highest.
Blessed is the One
who comes in the name of the Lord.
Hosanna in the highest.

Holy are you, and blessed is Jesus Christ,
in whom your Word became flesh
and came to dwell among us.
Through Jesus' suffering and death
you destroyed the power of sin and death.
You raised from the dead this same Jesus,
who now reigns with you in glory,
and poured upon us your Holy Spirit,
making us
the people of your new covenant.

On the night before meeting with death
Jesus took bread,
gave thanks to you,
broke the bread,
gave it to the disciples, and said:
"Take, eat;
this is my body which is given for you.
Do this in remembrance of me."

When the supper was over
Jesus took the cup,
gave thanks to you,
gave it to the disciples, and said:

"Drink from this, all of you;
this is my blood of the new covenant,
poured out for you and for many
for the forgiveness of sins.
Do this, as often as you drink it,
in remembrance of me."

And so, in remembrance
of these your mighty acts in Jesus Christ,
we offer ourselves
in praise and thanksgiving
as a holy and living sacrifice,
in union with Christ's offering for us,
as we proclaim the mystery of faith.

Christ has died,
Christ is risen,
Christ will come again.

Pour out your Holy Spirit on us,
gathered here,
and on these gifts of bread and wine.
Make them be for us
the body and blood of Christ,
that in unity we may be for the world
the body of Christ,
redeemed by Christ's blood,
until Christ comes in final victory
and we feast at your table for ever.

Through Christ, with Christ, in Christ,
in the unity of the Holy Spirit,
all honor and glory is yours,
Almighty God, now and for ever.

Amen.

And now,
with the confidence of children of God,
let us pray:

Our Father. . . .

Continue on page 43, 45, or 58.

Services 18 and 19 are intended for use in home or
hospital settings or in other situations where brevity
is essential.

Lift up your heart(s)
and give thanks to God.

Blessed are you, O God,
who with your Word and Holy Spirit
created all things and called them good.
In Jesus Christ your Word became flesh
and came to dwell among us.
Through Jesus' suffering and death
you destroyed the power of sin and death.
You raised from the dead this same Jesus,
who now reigns with you in glory,
and poured upon us your Holy Spirit,
making us
the people of your new covenant.

On the night before meeting with death
Jesus took bread,
gave thanks to you,
broke the bread,
gave it to the disciples, and said:
"Take, eat;
this is my body which is given for you.
Do this in remembrance of me."

When the supper was over
Jesus took the cup,
gave thanks to you,
gave it to the disciples, and said:
"Drink from this, all of you;
this is my blood of the new covenant,
poured out for you and for many
for the forgiveness of sins.
Do this, as often as you drink it,
in remembrance of me."

And so, in remembrance
of these your mighty acts in Jesus Christ,
we offer ourselves
in praise and thanksgiving
as a holy and living sacrifice
in union with Christ's offering for us.

Pour out your Holy Spirit on us
and on these gifts of bread and wine.
Make them be for us
the body and blood of Christ
that in unity we may be for the world
the body of Christ,

redeemed by Christ's blood,
until Christ comes in final victory
and we feast at your table for ever.

Through Christ, with Christ, in Christ,
in the unity of the Holy Spirit,
all honor and glory is yours,
Almighty God, now and for ever.

Amen.

And now,
with the confidence of children of God,
let us pray:

**Our Father in heaven,
hallowed be your Name,
your kingdom come,
your will be done
on earth as in heaven.
Give us today our daily bread.
Forgive us our sins
as we forgive those who sin against us.
Save us from the time of trial,
and deliver us from evil.
For the kingdom, the power, and the glory
are yours now and for ever. Amen.**

The minister breaks the bread.

*The bread and wine are given to the people,
with these or other words being exchanged:*
The body of Christ, given for you. **Amen.**
The blood of Christ, given for you. **Amen.**

*When all have received,
the Lord's table is put in order.*

*The minister may then give thanks
after Communion.*

A hymn or song may be sung.

The minister gives the blessing:
The grace of the Lord Jesus Christ,
and the love of God,
and the communion of the Holy Spirit
be with you all. **Amen.**

God be with you.
And also with you.
Lift up your hearts.
We lift them up to God.
Let us give thanks to the Almighty God.
It is right to give our thanks and praise.

It is right, and a good and joyful thing,
always and everywhere
to give thanks to you,
Sovereign of the Ages,
whose strong and loving arms
embrace the universe,
for with your eternal Word and Holy Spirit
you are for ever one God.

You created all things
and called them good.
You formed us in your image
and breathed into us the breath of life.
When we turned away, and our love failed,
your love remained steadfast.
You delivered us from captivity,
made covenant to be our sovereign God,
and spoke to us through your prophets.

And so, with your people on earth
and all the company of heaven,
we praise your name
and join their unending hymn:

Holy, holy, holy Lord,
God of power and might,
heaven and earth are full of your glory.
Hosanna in the highest.
Blessed is the One
who comes in the name of the Lord.
Hosanna in the highest.

Holy are you,
and blessed is your eternal Word,
who became flesh
and came to dwell among us
in Jesus Christ:
whom your Spirit anointed
to preach good news to the poor,
to proclaim release to the captives
and recovering of sight to the blind,

to set at liberty those who are oppressed,
and to announce that the time had come
when you would save your people;
who healed the sick, fed the hungry,
and ate with sinners.

By the baptism of Jesus' suffering,
death, and resurrection,
you gave birth to your Church,
delivered us from slavery to sin and death,
and made with us a new covenant
by water and the Spirit.
Jesus ascended with the promise
to be with us always,
in the power of your Word and Holy Spirit.

On the night before meeting with death,
Jesus took bread,
gave thanks to you,
broke the bread,
gave it to the disciples, and said:
"Take, eat;
this is my body which is given for you.
Do this in remembrance of me."

When the supper was over
Jesus took the cup,
gave thanks to you,
gave it to the disciples, and said:
"Drink from this, all of you;
this is my blood of the new covenant,
poured out for you and for many
for the forgiveness of sins.
Do this, as often as you drink it,
in remembrance of me."

And so, in remembrance
of these your mighty acts in Jesus Christ,
we offer ourselves
in praise and thanksgiving
as a holy and living sacrifice,
in union with Christ's offering for us,
as we proclaim the mystery of faith.

Christ has died,
Christ is risen,
Christ will come again.

Pour out your Holy Spirit on us,
gathered here,
and on these gifts of bread and wine.
Make them be for us
the body and blood of Christ,
that we may be for the world
the body of Christ,
redeemed by his blood.

By your Spirit make us one with Christ,
one with each other,
and one in ministry to all the world,
until Christ comes in final victory
and we feast at Christ's heavenly banquet.

Through your eternal Word Jesus Christ,
with the Holy Spirit in your holy Church,
all honor and glory is yours,
Almighty God, now and for ever.

Amen.

And now,
with the confidence of children of God,
let us pray:

Our Father in heaven, *(Abba,)*
hallowed be your Name,
your kingdom come, *(your reign begin,)*
your will be done
on earth as in heaven.
Give us today our daily bread.
Forgive us our sins
as we forgive those who sin against us.
Save us in the time of trial,
and deliver us from evil.
For the kingdom *(reign),*
the power, and the glory
are yours now and for ever. Amen.

The minister breaks the bread in silence,
or while saying:
Because there is one loaf,
we, who are many, are one body,
for we all partake of the one loaf.
The bread which we break
is a sharing in the body of Christ.

The minister lifts the cup in silence,
or while saying:
The cup over which we give thanks
is a sharing in the blood of Christ.

The bread and wine are given to the people,
with these or other words being exchanged:
The body of Christ, given for you. **Amen.**
The blood of Christ, given for you. **Amen.**

The congregation sings hymns
while the bread and cup are given.

When all have received,
the Lord's table is put in order.

The following prayer is then offered
by the minister or by all:
Eternal God,
we give you thanks for this holy mystery
in which you have given yourself to us.
Grant that we may go into the world
in the strength of your Spirit,
to give ourselves to others,
in Jesus' name. Amen.

A hymn or song may be sung.

The people are dismissed with the blessing:
Go forth in peace.
The grace of Jesus Christ,
and the love of God,
and the communion of the Holy Spirit
be with you all.

Amen.

For alternative texts following this Great Thanksgiving, turn to page 58.

The Lord be with you.
And also with you.
Lift up your hearts.
We lift them to the Lord.
Let us give thanks to the Lord our God.
It is right to give our thanks and praise.

It is indeed right
that we should praise you, gracious God,
for you created all things.
You formed us in your own image:
male and female you created us.
When we turned away from you in sin,
you did not cease to care for us,
but opened a path of salvation
for all people.
You made a covenant with Israel,
and through your servants
Abraham and Sarah
gave the promise of a blessing
to all nations.
Through Moses you led your people
from bondage to freedom;
through the prophets you renewed
your promise of salvation.

Therefore, with them,
and with all your saints
who have served you in every age,
we give thanks and raise our voices
to proclaim the glory of your name.

Holy, holy, holy Lord,
God of power and might,
heaven and earth are full of your glory.
Hosanna in the highest.
Blessed is he
who comes in the name of the Lord.
Hosanna in the highest.

Holy God, source of life and goodness,
all creation rightly gives you praise.
In the fullness of time,
you sent your Son Jesus Christ,
to share our human nature,
to live and die as one of us,
to reconcile us to you,
the God and Father of all.

He healed the sick,
and ate and drank
with outcasts and sinners;
he opened the eyes of the blind
and proclaimed the good news
of your kingdom
to the poor and to those in need.
In all things he fulfilled
your gracious will.

On the night
he freely gave himself to death,
our Lord Jesus Christ took bread,
and when he had given thanks to you,
he broke it, and gave it to his disciples,
and said, "Take, eat:
this is my body which is given for you.
Do this for the remembrance of me."

After supper he took the cup of wine;
and when he had given thanks,
he gave it to them,
and said, "Drink from this, all of you:
this is my blood of the new covenant,
which is shed for you and for many
for the forgiveness of sins.
Whenever you drink it,
do this for the remembrance of me."

Gracious God,
his perfect sacrifice
destroys the power of sin and death;
by raising him to life
you give us life for evermore.
Therefore we proclaim the mystery of faith.

Christ has died,
Christ is risen,
Christ will come again.

Recalling his death,
proclaiming his resurrection,
and looking for his coming again in glory,
we offer you, Father,
this bread and this cup.
Send your Holy Spirit upon us

and upon these gifts,
that all who eat and drink at this table
may be one body and one holy people,
a living sacrifice in Jesus Christ,
our Lord.

Through Christ, with Christ, and in Christ,
in the unity of the Holy Spirit,
all glory is yours, almighty Father,
now and for ever.

Amen.

And now,
with the confidence of children of God,
let us pray:

**Our Father in heaven,
hallowed be your Name,
your kingdom come,
your will be done
on earth as in heaven.
Give us today our daily bread.
Forgive us our sins
as we forgive those who sin against us.
Save us in the time of trial,
and deliver us from evil.
For the kingdom, the power, and the glory
are yours now and for ever. Amen.**

*The minister breaks the bread in silence,
or while saying:*
Because there is one loaf,
we, who are many, are one body,
for we all partake of the one loaf.
The bread which we break
is a sharing in the body of Christ.

*The minister lifts the cup in silence,
or while saying:*
The cup over which we give thanks
is a sharing in the blood of Christ.

*The bread and wine are given to the people,
with these or other words being exchanged:*
The body of Christ, given for you. **Amen.**
The blood of Christ, given for you. **Amen.**

*The congregation sings hymns
while the bread and cup are given.*

*When all have received,
the Lord's table is put in order.*

*The following prayer is then offered
by the minister or by all:*
**Loving God, we thank you
that you have fed us in this Sacrament,
united us with Christ,
and given us a foretaste
of your heavenly banquet.
Send us out in the power of your Spirit
to live and work to your praise and glory,
in Jesus' name. Amen.**

A hymn or song may be sung.

The people are dismissed with the blessing:
Go forth in peace.
The grace of Jesus Christ,
and the love of God,
and the communion of the Holy Spirit
be with you all.

Amen.

For alternative texts following this Great Thanksgiving, turn to page 58.

The Lord be with you.
And also with you.
Lift up your hearts.
We lift them to the Lord.
Let us give thanks to the Lord our God.
It is right to give God thanks and praise.

We thank you, God,
Father and Mother of us all.
From the beginning you made the world
and all its creatures;
you made people to live for you
and for each other.
We praise you, God.

You created Adam and Eve
and gave them a garden;
You showed Noah a rainbow;
You gave strength to Moses
to free his people
and taught Miriam to sing;
You gave courage to Esther
and loyalty to Ruth.
You helped David defeat the giant
and gave him a harp to sing with.
We praise you, God.

And yet even they turned away from you
and forgot about you, as we do too.
But you did not forget.
You sent your only child Jesus to the world
to show how much you love us
and to bring us back to you again
We praise you, God.

As one of us he came,
at first a tender infant,
then a child, a youth and an adult.
He rejoiced with those who rejoiced
and wept with those who wept.
To the despairing he spoke a word of hope.
To the sick he gave healing.
To the rejected he was a friend.
And yet he was betrayed
and nailed to a cross.
But he was lifted from the grave
and restored to life,

that he might be with us
and we with him
Alive for evermore!
Therefore, with all the saints,
and with angels in the heavens,
our hearts beat with happiness and we sing

Holy, holy, holy Lord,
God of power and might.
Heaven and earth are full of your glory.
Hosanna in the highest.
Blessed is the one
who comes in the name of the Lord
Hosanna in the highest.

On the night before Jesus died,
he had supper with his disciples:
he took bread;
thanked you, as we have thanked you;
broke the bread;
and gave the bread to his friends, saying,
"Take this, all of you, and eat it.
This is my body, given for you.
Each time you do this, remember me."
After supper he took the wine;
thanked you for it,
and passed a cup of wine to his friends,
saying, "This cup is the new promise
God has made with you in my blood.
Each time you do this
and drink from this cup,
remember me."

Remembering his death
and celebrating his resurrection,
we await with hope his coming again
to bring peace and justice to the earth.
Come, Lord Jesus.

We pray you, God of Love,
send your Holy Spirit
upon us and what we do here
that we, and these gifts,
touched by your Spirit,
may be signs of life and love
to each other, and to all the world.

Through Christ, with Christ, and in Christ,
in the unity of the Holy Spirit,
all glory is yours, God most holy,
now and for ever.
Amen.

And now,
with the confidence of children of God,
let us pray:

Our Father in heaven,
hallowed be your Name,
your kingdom come,
your will be done
on earth as in heaven.
Give us today our daily bread.
Forgive us our sins
as we forgive those who sin against us.
Save us from the time of trial,
and deliver us from evil.
For the kingdom, the power, and the glory
are yours now and for ever. Amen.

The minister breaks the bread
and then lifts the cup,
in silence, or while saying:
These are gifts from God
for you the people of God.

The bread and wine are given to the people,
with these or other words being exchanged:
The body of Christ, given for you. **Amen.**
The blood of Christ, given for you. **Amen.**

The congregation sings hymns
while the bread and cup are given.

When all have received,
The Lord's table is put in order.

The following prayer is then offered
by the minister or by all:
Most loving God,
we thank you for giving us Jesus
and sharing with us in his holy meal.
This time together
helps us to grow as his disciples.
Now we go out with you
to give ourselves to others,
in Jesus' name. Amen.

A hymn or song may be sung.

The people are dismissed with the blessing:
Go forth in peace.
The grace of the Lord Jesus Christ,
and the love of God,
and the communion of the Holy Spirit
be with you all.

Amen.

While all services in this book assume that children may be present in the congregation, Service 22 is designed for occasions when a special attempt is being made to help children become familiar with Holy Communion. This text may be varied to focus upon Bible stories with which the children are familiar.

Lift up your hearts.
We lift them to the Lord.
Let us give thanks to the Lord our God.
It is right to give God thanks and praise.

It is right and good to give you thanks,
Almighty God,
for you are the source of light and life.
You made us in your image
and called us to new life
in Jesus Christ.
In all times and places
your people proclaim your glory
in unending praise:

Holy, holy, holy Lord,
God of power and might,
heaven and earth are full of your glory.
Hosanna in the highest.
Blessed is the one
who comes in the name of the Lord.
Hosanna in the highest.

We remember with joy the grace
by which you created all things
and made us in your own image.
We rejoice
that you called a people in covenant
to be a light to the nations.
Yet we rebelled against your will.
In spite of the prophets and pastors
sent forth to us,
we continued to break your covenant.

In the fullness of time,
you sent your only Son to save us.
Incarnate by the Holy Spirit,
born of your favored one, Mary,
sharing our life,
he reconciled us to your love.
At the Jordan
your Spirit descended upon him,
anointing him
to preach the good news of your reign.
He healed the sick and fed the hungry,
manifesting the power of your compassion.
He sought out the lost
and broke bread with sinners,

witnessing the fullness of your grace.
We beheld his glory.

On the night before he died for us,
Jesus took bread;
giving thanks to you,
he broke the bread
and offered it to his disciples, saying:
"Take this and eat;
this is my body which is given for you,
do this in remembrance of me."

Taking a cup,
again he gave thanks to you,
shared the cup with his disciples and said:
"This is the cup of the new covenant
in my blood.
Drink from this all of you.
This is poured out for you and for many,
for the forgiveness of sins."

After the meal our Lord was arrested,
abandoned by his followers and beaten.
He stood trial
and was put to death on a cross.
Having emptied himself
in the form of a servant,
and being obedient even to death,
he was raised from the dead
and exalted as Lord of heaven and earth.
Through him you bestow
the gift of your Spirit,
uniting your Church,
empowering its mission,
and leading us into the new creation
you have promised.

Gracious God, we celebrate with joy
the redemption won for us in Jesus Christ.
Grant that in praise and thanksgiving
we may be a living sacrifice,
holy and acceptable in your sight,
that our lives may proclaim
the mystery of faith:

Christ has died,
Christ is risen,
Christ will come again.

Loving God,
pour out your Holy Spirit upon us
and upon these gifts,
that they may be for us the body and blood
of our Savior Jesus Christ.
Grant that we may be for the world
the body of Christ,
redeemed through his blood,
serving and reconciling all people to you.

Remember your Church,
scattered upon the face of the earth;
gather it in unity
and preserve it in truth.
Remember the saints
who have gone before us
especially _____ and _____.
(Here may occur special names.)
In communion with them
and with all creation,
we worship and glorify you always:

Through your Son Jesus Christ
with the Holy Spirit in your Holy Church,
all glory and honor is yours,
Almighty God, now and for ever. Amen.

And now,
with the confidence of children of God,
let us pray:
. . . .
Our Father in heaven,
hallowed be your Name,
your kingdom come,
your will be done
on earth as in heaven.
Give us today our daily bread.
Forgive us our sins
as we forgive those who sin against us.
Save us from the time of trial,
and deliver us from evil.
For the kingdom, the power, and the glory
are yours now and for ever. Amen.
. . . .
(The minister breaks the bread in silence
or while saying:)
The bread which we break,
is it not a sharing in the body of Christ?

Because there is one bread,
we who are many are one body,
for we all partake of the one bread.

The wine which we drink,
is it not a sharing in the blood of Christ?

The cup which we bless
is the communion in the blood of Christ.

The bread and the cup are shared.

One of the following prayers
is offered in closing:

Bountiful God, we give thanks
that you have refreshed us at your table
by granting us the presence of Christ.
Strengthen our faith,
increase our love for one another,
and send us forth into the world
in courage and peace,
rejoicing in the power of the Holy Spirit.
Amen.

God our help,
we thank you for this supper
shared in the Spirit
with your servant Jesus,
who makes us new and strong,
who brings life eternal.
We praise you for giving us all good gifts
and pledge ourselves to serve you,
even as in Christ you have served us.
Amen.

Here a hymn or song may be sung.

The people are dismissed with the blessing:
The grace of the Lord Jesus Christ
and the love of God
and the communion of the Holy Spirit
be with you all.
Amen.

Service 21 has been prepared by the Consultation on
Church Union (COCU) and is especially suited to
ecumenical occasions. Since a translation of the
Lord's Prayer is not provided in this service, the
International Consultation on English Texts version
has been added.

The Lord be with you.
And also with you.
Lift up your hearts.
We lift them to the Lord.
Let us give thanks to the Lord our God.
It is right to give him thanks and praise.

Truly it is right and good to glorify you,
at all times and in all places,
to offer you our thanksgiving O Lord,
Holy Father,
Almighty and Everlasting God.

Through your living Word
you created all things
and pronounced them good.
You made human beings
in your own image,
to share your life and reflect your glory.
When the time had fully come,
you gave Christ to us
as the Way, the Truth and the Life.
He accepted baptism and consecration
as your Servant
to announce the good news to the poor.
At the last supper
Christ bequeathed to us the eucharist,
that we should celebrate
the memorial of the cross and resurrection,
and receive his presence as food.
To all the redeemed
Christ gave the royal priesthood
and, in loving his brothers and sisters,
chooses those who share in the ministry,
that they may feed the Church
with your Word
and enable it to live by your Sacraments.

Wherefore, Lord,
with the angels and all the saints,
we proclaim and sing your glory:

Holy, holy, holy Lord,
God of power and might,
heaven and earth are full of your glory.
Hosanna in the highest.
Blessed is he
who comes in the name of the Lord.
Hosanna in the highest.

O God, Lord of the universe, you are holy
and your glory is beyond measure.
Upon your eucharist
send the life-giving Spirit,
who spoke by Moses and the Prophets,
who overshadowed the Virgin Mary
with grace,
who descended upon Jesus
in the river Jordan
and upon the Apostles
on the day of Pentecost.
May the outpouring of this Spirit of Fire
transfigure this thanksgiving meal
that this bread and wine
may become for us
the body and blood of Christ.

Veni Creator Spiritus!
[*or,* **Come, Creator Spirit!**]

May this Creator Spirit
accomplish the words of your beloved Son,
who, in the night in which he was betrayed,
took bread,
and when he had given thanks to you,
broke it
and gave it to his disciples, saying:
Take, eat:
this is my body, which is given for you.
Do this for the remembrance of me.

After supper he took the cup
and when he had given thanks,
he gave it to them and said:
Drink this, all of you:
this is my blood of the new covenant,
which is shed for you and for many
for the forgiveness of sins.
Do this for the remembrance of me.

Great is the mystery of faith.

Your death, Lord Jesus, we proclaim!
Your resurrection we celebrate!
Your coming in glory we await!

Wherefore, Lord, we celebrate today
the memorial of our redemption:
we recall
the birth and life of your Son among us,
his baptism by John,
his last meal with the apostles,
his death
and descent to the abode of the dead;
we proclaim Christ's resurrection
and ascension in glory,
where as our Great High Priest
he ever intercedes for all people;
and we look for his coming at the last.

United in Christ's priesthood,
we present to you this memorial:
Remember the sacrifice of your Son
and grant to people everywhere
the benefits of Christ's redemptive work.

Maranatha, the Lord comes!

Behold, Lord, this eucharist
which you yourself gave to the Church
and graciously receive it,
as you accept the offering of your Son
whereby we are reinstated
in your Covenant.
As we partake of Christ's body and blood,
fill us with the Holy Spirit
that we may be one single body
and one single spirit in Christ,
a living sacrifice
to the praise of your glory.

Veni Creator Spiritus!
[or, Come, Creator Spirit!]

Remember, Lord, your one,
holy, catholic and apostolic Church,
redeemed by the blood of Christ.
Reveal its unity,
guard its faith,
and preserve it in peace.
Remember, Lord,
all the servants of your Church:
bishops, presbyters, deacons,
and all to whom you have given
special gifts of ministry.

(Remember especially. . . .)
Remember also all our sisters and brothers
who have died in the peace of Christ,
and those whose faith
is known to you alone:
guide them to the joyful feast
prepared for all peoples in your presence,
with the blessed Virgin Mary,
with the patriarchs and prophets,
the apostles and martyrs. . .
and all the saints
for whom your friendship was life.

With all these we sing your praise
and await the happiness of your Kingdom
where with the whole creation,
finally delivered from sin and death,
we shall be enabled to glorify you
through Christ our Lord;

Maranatha, the Lord comes!

Through Christ, with Christ, in Christ,
all honor and glory is yours,
Almighty God and Father,
in the unity of the Holy Spirit,
now and for ever.

Amen.

United by one baptism
in the same Holy Spirit
and the same Body of Christ,
we pray as God's sons and daughters:
· · · · · · · · · ·

Our Father in heaven,
hallowed be your name,
your kingdom come,
your will be done,
on earth as in heaven.
Give us today our daily bread.
Forgive us our sins,
as we forgive those who sin against us.
Save us from the time of trial,
and deliver us from evil.
For the kingdom, the power, and the glory
are yours now and for ever. Amen.

· · · · · · · · · ·

The Lima Liturgy continues on the next page.

Lord Jesus Christ, you told your apostles:
Peace I leave with you,
my peace I give to you.
Look not on our sins
but on the faith of your Church.
In order that your will be done,
grant us always this peace
and guide us towards the perfect unity
of your Kingdom for ever.

Amen.

The peace of the Lord be with you always.

And also with you.

Let us give one another
a sign of reconciliation and peace.

The Peace is exchanged.

As the bread is broken:
The bread which we break
is the communion of the Body of Christ,
the cup of blessing
for which we give thanks
is the communion in the Blood of Christ.

**Lamb of God,
you take away the sins of the world,
have mercy on us.
Lamb of God,
you take aways the sins of the world,
have mercy on us.
Lamb of God,
you take away the sins of the world,
grant us peace.**

The bread and cup are given to the people.

The following prayer is then offered:
In peace let us pray to the Lord:
O Lord our God,
we give you thanks
for uniting us by baptism
in the Body of Christ
and for filling us with joy
in the eucharist.

Lead us towards the full visible unity
of your Church
and help us to treasure
all the signs of reconciliation
you have granted us.
Now that we have tasted of
the banquet you have prepared for us
in the world to come,
may we all one day share together
the inheritance of the saints
in the life of your heavenly city,
through Jesus Christ, your Son, our Lord,
who lives and reigns with you
in the unity of the Holy Spirit,
ever one God, world without end.

Amen.

A final hymn is sung.

A word of mission is given.

The people are dismissed with the blessing:
The Lord bless you and keep you.
The Lord make his face to shine on you
and be gracious to you.
The Lord look upon you with favor
and give you peace.
Almighty God,
Father, Son and Holy Spirit,
bless you now and forever.

Amen.

This service was prepared by the Faith and Order Commission of the World Council of Churches and was first used at its meeting on January 15, 1982, in Lima, Peru. It has since been used on many other ecumenical occasions, including the Sixth Assembly of the World Council of Churches in Vancouver, with the Archbishop of Canterbury as the presiding celebrant. As the Lord's Prayer is not included in the Lima Liturgy, the International Consultation on English Texts version has been added.

WORDS AT GIVING THE BREAD AND CUP

1

The body of Christ, given for you. **Amen.**
The blood of Christ, given for you. **Amen.**

2

Name, the body of Christ, given for you.
Amen.
Name, the blood of Christ, given for you.
Amen.

3

The body of Christ, the bread of heaven.
Amen.
The blood of Christ, the cup of salvation.
Amen.

4

Jesus Christ, the bread of heaven. **Amen.**
Jesus Christ, the cup of salvation. **Amen.**

5

The body of Christ. **Amen.**
The blood of Christ. **Amen.**

6

Name, body of Christ. **Amen.**
Name, blood of Christ. **Amen.**

AN ANCIENT PRAYER

The following rubric and prayer is from the *Didache (The Teaching of the Twelve Apostles)* which dates from the late first or early second century. It is uncertain whether the liturgy of which it is a part belongs to a love feast *(agape)* or to Holy Communion. In either event, this prayer may appropriately be prayed after Communion. See also page 43.

And after you have had your fill,
give thanks thus:
We give thanks to you, holy Father,
for your holy name
which you have enshrined in our hearts,
and for the knowledge and faith
and immortality
which you have made known to us
through your child Jesus;
glory to you for evermore.
You, Lord Almighty, created all things
for the sake of your name
and gave food and drink
to men [humanity]
for their enjoyment,
that they might give you thanks;
but to us
you have granted spiritual food and drink
for eternal life through your child Jesus.
Above all we give you thanks
because you are mighty;
glory to you for evermore.
Amen.

THE LORD'S PRAYER: ALTERNATE VERSIONS

And now,
with the confidence of children of God,
let us pray:

1

Our Father in heaven,
hallowed be your name,
your kingdom come,
your will be done,
on earth as in heaven.
Give us today our daily bread.
Forgive us our sins
as we forgive those who sin against us.
Save us from the time of trial
and deliver us from evil.
For the kingdom, the power, and the glory
are yours now and for ever. Amen.

2

Our Father, who art in heaven,
hallowed be thy name.
Thy kingdom come,
thy will be done
on earth as it is in heaven.
Give us this day our daily bread.
And forgive us our trespasses,
as we forgive those
who trespass against us.
And lead us not into temptation,
but deliver us from evil.
For thine is the kingdom,
and the power, and the glory,
forever. Amen.

3

Our Father, who art in heaven;
hallowed be thy name;
thy kingdom come,
thy will be done,
on earth as it is in heaven.
Give us this day our daily bread;
and forgive us our debts
as we forgive our debtors.
And lead us not into temptation
but deliver us from evil.
For thine is the kingdom,
and the power, and the glory,
forever. Amen.

WORDS AT BREAKING THE BREAD

The minister breaks the bread in silence and then lifts the cup in silence or while saying any of the following sets of sentences.

1

Because there is one loaf,
we, who are many, are one body,
for we all partake of the one loaf.
The bread which we break
is a sharing in the body of Christ.

The cup over which we give thanks
is a sharing in the blood of Christ.

2

Through the broken bread
we participate in the body of Christ.

Through the cup of blessing
we participate in the new life
Christ gives.

3

[Alleluia.]
Christ our Passover is sacrificed for us;
Therefore let us keep the feast.
[Alleluia.]

4

The Gifts of God for the People of God.

5

The body of our Lord Jesus Christ,
given for you,
preserve your souls and bodies
to everlasting life.

The blood of our Lord Jesus Christ,
given for you,
preserve your souls and bodies
to everlasting life.

6

Take and eat this
in remembrance of Christ,
and feed on him in your hearts
by faith with thanksgiving.

Drink this in remembrance of Christ
and be thankful.

PRAYERS AFTER COMMUNION

1

Eternal God,
we give you thanks for this holy mystery
in which you have given yourself to us.
Grant that we may go into the world
in the strength of your Spirit,
to give ourselves to others,
in the name of Jesus Christ our Lord.
Amen.

2

You have given yourself to us, Lord.
Now we give ourselves for others.
Your love has made us a new people;
**as a people of love
we will serve you with joy.**
Your glory has filled our hearts;
**Help us to glorify you in all things.
Amen.**

3

Most loving God,
you have given us a share
in the one bread and the one cup
and made us one in Christ.
Help us to bring your salvation and joy
to all the world.
We ask this through Christ our Lord.
Amen.

4

Bountiful God, we give thanks
that you have refreshed us at your table
by granting us the presence of Christ.
Strengthen our faith,
increase our love for one another,
and send us forth into the world,
in courage and peace,
rejoicing in the power of the Holy Spirit.
Amen.

*The closing hymn may also serve as the
prayer after Communion. Examples include:*
"For the Bread, Which Thou Hast Broken"
"Author of Life Divine"
"Now Thank We All Our God"
"Now Let Us from This Table Rise"
A doxology or doxological stanza

BLESSINGS (BENEDICTIONS)

1

Go forth in peace.
The grace of the Lord Jesus Christ,
and the love of God,
and the communion of the Holy Spirit
be with you all. **Amen.**

2

The peace of God,
which passeth all understanding,
keep your hearts and minds
in the knowledge and love of God,
and of his Son Jesus Christ our Lord;
and the blessing of God Almighty,
the Father, the Son, and the Holy Spirit,
be among you, and remain with you always.
Amen.

3

Go forth in peace, and be of good courage;
hold fast that which is good,
rejoicing in the power of the Holy Spirit.
And the blessing of God,
Father, Son, and Holy Spirit,
be with you and remain with you for ever.
Amen.

4

Now may the God of peace
who brought again from the dead
our Lord Jesus,
the great shepherd of the sheep,
by the blood of the eternal covenant,
equip you with everything good
that you may do his will,
working in you
that which is pleasing in his sight,
through Jesus Christ:
to whom be glory for ever and ever.
Amen.

5

The Lord bless you and keep you:
The Lord make his face shine on you
and be gracious to you:
The Lord lift up his countenance
upon you,
and give you peace. **Amen.**

SOURCES

Pages 6–7, 9. Adapted from *The Book of Services*, The United Methodist Church (Nashville: The United Methodist Publishing House, 1985). (Hereafter BOS.)

Page 8. Adapted from *The Book of Common Prayer*, the Episcopal Church (New York: Seabury, 1979) and BOS.

Page 10. "The Great Thanksgiving: Its Essential Elements" is adapted from the chapter of the same title in *Word and Table*, 1st ed. (Nashville: Abingdon, 1976).

Page 11. *Eucharistic Prayer of Hippolytus* (Washington, D.C.: International Commission on English in the Liturgy, 1983). Minor adaptations made.

The texts for the Sursum Corda, the Sanctus and Benedictus, and the Lord's Prayer used throughout this book (except for texts 2 and 3 on page 58) are taken or adapted from *Prayers We Have in Common*, International Consultation on English Texts, 2nd rev. ed. (Philadelphia: Fortress, 1976).

The acclamation "Christ has died, Christ is risen, Christ will come again" used throughout this book is from the English translation of *The Roman Missal*, International Committee on English in the Liturgy, Inc., 1973.

The prayer "Loving God..." on pages 13, 17, 19, 21, 25, 27, 29, 33, 35, 37, and 49 is adapted from *The Service for the Lord's Day* (Supplemental Liturgical Resource 1), the Joint Office of Worship for the Presbyterian Church (U.S.A.) and the Cumberland Presbyterian Church (Philadelphia: Westminster, 1984).

Services 1–3. Adapted from BOS.

Services 4–14. The Great Thanksgivings are taken or adapted from *Handbook of the Christian Year*, by Hoyt L. Hickman, Don E. Saliers, Lawrence H. Stookey, and James F. White (Nashville: Abingdon, 1986). The remainder of the services is from BOS. Brackets added in places.

Services 15–16. BOS.

Service 17. "Great Thanksgiving" by Hoyt Hickman. The sentence "As a mother..." is from Eucharistic Prayer A (Washington: International Committee on English in the Liturgy, 1986). The sentence "As the grain..." is freely adapted from the *Didache* in *Prayers of the Eucharist*, trans. and ed. by R. C. D. Jasper and G. J. Cuming (London: Collins, 1975). Other texts from BOS.

Services 18–20. Adapted from BOS.

Service 21. Great Thanksgiving is Eucharistic Prayer 1 in *The Book of Alternative Services of the Anglican Church of Canada* (Toronto: Anglican Book Centre, 1985). Other texts from BOS.

Service 22. Great Thanksgiving adapted from Eucharistic Prayer VII in *A Sunday Liturgy for Optional Use in The United Church of Canada* (Toronto: The United Church of Canada, 1984). Other texts from BOS and by Hoyt Hickman.

Service 23. Adapted from *The Sacrament of the Lord's Supper: A New Text 1984*, Consultation on Church Union, 1984. The Lord's Prayer from *Prayers We Have in Common*, International Consultation on English Texts, 1975.

Service 24. From "The Eucharistic Liturgy of Lima" in *Baptism and Eucharist*, ed. by Max Thurian and Geoffrey Wainwright (Geneva: World Council of Churches Publications, 1983; Grand Rapids, Eerdmans, 1983). The Lord's Prayer from *Prayers We Have in Common*, International Consultation on English texts, 1975.

Words at Giving the Bread and Cup.
1. BOS.
2. BOS, adapted.
3. *The Book of Common Prayer*.
4. Adapted from *An Order of Worship*, Consultation on Church Union (Cincinnati, OH: Forward Movement Publications, 1968).
5. *The Roman Missal*, International Committee on English in the Liturgy, Inc., 1973.

An Ancient Prayer. The *Didache (The Teaching of the Twelve Apostles)* in *Prayers of the Eucharist: Early and Reformed*, trans. and ed. by R. C. D. Jasper and G. J. Cuming (London: Collins, 1975).

The Lord's Prayer
1. *Prayers We Have in Common*, International Consultation on English Texts, 1975.
2. *Ritual of The United Methodist Church*, The United Methodist Church (Nashville: United Methodist Publishing House, 1964).
3. *The Discipline of The Evangelical United Brethren Church*, The Evangelical United Brethren Church (Harrisburg, PA: The Evangelical Press, 1959; Dayton, OH: The Otterbein Press, 1959).

Words at Breaking the Bread
1. BOS.
2. *The Hymnal of the United Church of Christ*, the United Church of Christ (Philadelphia: United Church Press, 1974).
3 and 4. *The Book of Common Prayer*.
5 and 6. Adapted from *The Book of Worship for Church and Home*, The United Methodist Church (Nashville: United Methodist Publishing House, 1965).

Prayers After Communion
1 and 2. BOS.
3. *The Roman Missal*, International Committee on English in the Liturgy, Inc., 1973.
4. *The Sacrament of the Lord's Supper: A New Text 1984*, Consultation on Church Union, 1984.

Blessings (Benedictions)
1. Second sentence adapted from II Corinthians 13:14 (RSV).
2. *Ritual of The United Methodist Church*, The United Methodist Church (Nashville: United Methodist Publishing House, 1964).
3. *The Book of Worship for Church and Home* The United Methodist Church, (Nashville: United Methodist Publishing House, 1965).
4. Hebrews 13:20-21 (RSV).
5. Numbers 6:24-26 (adapted from RSV).